To Delaine
with best wishes
& I hope you

Al Gore Jr.
Born To Lead

enjoy al's story!

Hank Hillin

Best of all

1992

HANK HILLIN
AL GORE JR.
Born To Lead

PINE HALL PRESS
P.O. Box 150657
Nashville, TN 37215-0657

AL GORE JR.:Born to Lead

Copyright © 1988 by Hank Hillin

Manufactured by Curley Printing Company in Nashville, Tennessee in the United States of America.

PINE HALL PRESS
Post Office Box 150657
Nashville, Tennessee 37215-0657
(615) 298-3502

Printing and binding design by Ron Green and associates at Curley Printing Company, Nashville, Tennessee.

Typography by Michael Walker

Bookcover designed by Edison Communications

First Edition, June 1988

Library of Congress Cataloging-in-Publication Data

Hillin, Hank, 1930-
    Al Gore Jr.: born to lead

    Bibliography: p.
    Includes index.
    1. Gore, Albert, 1948-   . 2. Legislators–United States–Biography. 3. United States. Congress. Senate–Biography. 4. Presidential Candidates–United States–Biography. I. Title.
E840.8.G65H55 1988   328.73'092'4   88-5927
ISBN 0-9615022-1-5 (pbk.)

Dedicated to the memories of two outstanding Tennessee women.
Nancy Gore Hunger, Al Gore's sister.
Katie Batey Hillin, my mother.

Contents

Foreword

I like to be asked to do things involving people I like and respect and Al Gore and Hank Hillin are both friends in that category. Though Al was only with us here at *The Tennessean* about four years in the early 1970's, even then it was easy to see a brilliant future for him in journalism. Al was driven to do his best, to perform well, and didn't mind the hours or the work involved in digging out the facts of a story. Armed with great credibility and exceptional intelligence, Al Gore's name soon earned the trust of those of us here at the paper and that of the general public.

Though I understand that this biography was totally Hank Hillin's project, Al couldn't have picked a fairer or more thorough investigator to develop and report on his life. A young FBI agent in the Nashville office in the early 1960's when I first met him around the courthouses in Nashville, Hank was instrumental in ridding the city of bank robbery gangs that plagued our community the rest of that decade, then had outstanding success in battling political corruption and crooked politicians the last years of his bureau career.

I hope that it's not too long until the entire nation recognizes the leadership potential in Al Gore Jr., an outstanding young Tennessean.

Wayne Whitt
Managing Editor
The Tennessean

Al Gore endorses Mass. Gov. Michael Dukakis for president, Nashville, June 15, 1988 (photo by Larry McCormick, courtesy *Nashville Banner*)

Introduction

Several months before the announcement that he would seek the Democratic Party's nomination for president in the 1988 election, Al Gore Jr. appeared on "One on One," a talk show hosted by John McLaughlin for Public Television. Mr. McLaughlin, the internationally respected editor of the conservative *National Review*, opened the show with these remarks:

"You've got the magical name—Al Gore. Your father was in Congress for 32 years. You've got character. You've got no clay feet, no skeletons showing. You're intelligent. You're well-informed. You've got a Vietnam war record. You've been an investigative reporter, and you've got religious coloration, too. For one year, you were a divinity student and you're a devout Baptist. You're almost too good to be true. Are you too good to be true?" [1]

That's what Bill and Paula Cunningham wanted to know when I talked with them about Albert Gore Jr. months ago over lunch in Nashville. They're friends of mine, both writers, from western Kentucky, where Bill has acquired a well-deserved reputation as an honest, tough state prosecutor. During a lull in the conversation they mentioned that their governor-elect, Wallace Wilkinson, might endorse and support Al Gore, and wanted to know if he really was "too good to be true." They knew that I'd devoted the last five years of my twenty-six-year FBI career to fighting political corruption in Tennessee's most corrupt state administration, and both had helped promote in Kentucky the sale of my book that detailed that struggle.

"Are you sure Tennessee can produce an honest politician?" my lawyer-prosecutor friend asked, smiling. "How do you know he's as honest as he claims? Or, for that matter, who verifies what politicians say, except sometimes the press?" Bill turned in his chair, then looked directly at me, lowering his voice. "Could Al Gore have survived the same type of investigation you did on Governor Blanton's administration, or an applicant-type investigation the FBI conducts on high-level government appointees, Supreme Court justices and Cabinet members?"

In a flash, I decided I would investigate Gore, conduct a rigorous character inquiry of his background as close as possible to the type the Bureau conducts in high-level special inquiry matters, then report the results in a book.

My friend was waiting for my answer. "I don't know if he can or not. I'll let you know when I finish," I said.

Although I advised Senator Gore, his staff and family, of my intentions, I did not speak with him or anyone in his family or on his staff during the probe or during the writing of this book. The idea and the resulting book are my responsibility. The book is, in its totality, an "unauthorized biography."

The only agency in the world which can duplicate an FBI inquiry is the FBI itself, but I tried, spending months interviewing people who had known Al Gore at critical stages of his life and during the development of his character. I checked records and files in courthouses from Nashville-Carthage to Washington-Arlington. Political sources and reporters who have traveled with and written about him were interviewed, and sources available only to an ex-FBI agent with years of experience were queried.

I verified every residence Gore has ever had and reviewed every property transfer he has been involved in. I went to the subdivision he developed in Carthage and observed the construction of the homes.

I determined that he had no criminal record and there was no indication that he's ever had ties to or any connection with organized crime or any criminal activity. He's licensed by his home state to operate vehicles, including motorcycles, and though he has no known history of accidents or citations, my law enforcement sources tell me that, like his father, he has been observed to exceed posted speed limits and sometimes drives impatiently in heavy traffic situations.

He has done reasonably well financially. Given his natural ability, background and contacts, however, he could have acquired extensive wealth had he not gone into government. Currently, he owes about $1.4 million for campaign debts for which he personally signed notes. Inquiry tends to indicate his and Tipper's net worth at between $586,000 and $629,000, which includes their equity in Tennessee and Virginia real property, savings accounts, funds in a Senate credit union, $80,000 in zinc mineral rights, and Tipper's ownership of stock valued at $52,696. They have established trusts for their four children.

His taxable income dipped in 1987 to $131,783 from $133,550 in 1986, when he paid federal income taxes of $47,121. In 1987, his Senate salary jumped to $87,483 from $75,000 in 1986. He earned $30,040 in speaking honoraria in 1986; this figure dropped to $24,300 in 1987. Tipper received royalties of $5,654 in 1987 for her book *Raising PG Kids in an X-Rated Society.* In both years he and Tipper had mineral royalties and farm income and contributed the maximum allowed to an IRA. In 1986, itemized deductions for the Gores and their four children totalled $25,195, along with an additional exemption of $6,480 for family members.

The Gores' real property consists of a brick ranch home and 79 acres of farm land in Smith County, Tennessee, currently appraised at $110,000, and a house and lot in Arlington, Va., purchased for $150,000 on December 2, 1977, currently valued at $426,100.

No evidence of racial or social prejudice, bigotry or discrimination on his part was developed. Apparently the opposite is true, in fact. His roommate at Harvard was black and described him as totally unprejudiced, claiming that Gore taught him "not to be prejudiced myself."

You learn personal trivia during an investigation. For example, his favorite actor is Tommy Lee Jones, a friend from Texas who graduated with him from Harvard in 1969 and was in his wedding. His favorite actress is Meryl Streep.

He attends any George Strait or Bruce Springsteen concert he can get to, and his favorite albums are Bruce Springsteen's "Born in the USA" and Springsteen's "Live Album." He maintains the main problem with popular music today is that "a small percentage of it that contains violent lyrics that degrade women and glorify drugs is targeted at the younger and younger kids."

A radio and television news addict, he prefers National Public Radio, news weekly and science magazines. He enjoys James Michener's novels and David Halberstam's nonfiction writing.

Though he attempts to avoid them, he prefers foods rich in fats and cholesterol. He tries to eat fruits, vegetables and white meat. He tries to avoid drinks which contain caffeine. A physical fitness enthusiast, he tries to jog at least four miles each morning and occasionally plays tennis. He's an excellent swimmer and an outstanding waterskier, and participated in track, basketball and football during his high school years.

Extremely considerate and polite, Gore has been described as a country gentleman, exceptionally compassionate, relatively unaffected by fame and position. He dislikes any perception that any honor or achievement on his part came as a result of his father's thirty-two years as an important member of the House and Senate of the United States.

The most important thing I learned is that Al Gore Jr. has high character, outstanding integrity and an impeccable reputation. If being a devoted husband and father, a loyal friend, a hard worker, a highly intelligent and patriotic American makes you "too good to be true," then Al Gore is.

Hank Hillin
Route 2
Brentwood, Tennessee 37027
June, 1988

Chapter One

Almighty God, who has given us this good land for our heritage – Endue with the spirit of wisdom those to whom in thy name we entrust the authority of government that there may be justice and peace at home, and that, through obedience to thy law we may show forth thy praise among the nations of the earth. [1]

Charles Martin
Headmaster, St. Albans School
for Boys, 1949-1977

When he was twenty-eight, Al Gore became the youngest congressman ever elected from Tennessee's Fourth Congressional District, the same district that sent his father to the House of Representatives thirty-eight years earlier. Though he had earlier rejected a political career, he seized the opportunity once it came, and threw himself into his work as a member of the House of Representatives with reckless enthusiasm and unquestionable ability.

In the eight years that followed, he acquired national prominence as one of the most outstanding legislators Tennessee had ever sent to Congress.

When he was thirty-four, he suffered the first great loss of his life when his beloved sister, Nancy, died in the course of his campaign for the U.S. Senate seat that their father had occupied for eighteen years. Four months later, Tennessee showed the love and high esteem it felt for him and his family when he received the highest vote total any candidate had ever received in any statewide race in its history. Representative Al Gore Jr. had been promoted to Senator Al Gore Jr.

After he had been in the U.S. Senate two years, friends and political supporters urged him to consider a run at the Democratic nomination

Al Gore

Nancy Gore Hunger

for the presidency in 1988, but he refused even to consider the possibility until he felt he was ready to make a contribution to the process. As the debate heightened and the issues narrowed, the list from the Democratic Party side grew throughout 1986 and early 1987 to include front-runner Gary Hart, former U.S. senator from Colorado; U.S. Senator Joe Biden of Delaware; Governor Michael Dukakis of Massachusetts; U.S. Representative Richard Gephardt of Missouri; the Reverend Jesse Jackson of Chicago, Illinois; and U.S. Senator Paul Simon of Illinois.

* * *

In keeping with a tradition begun years earlier, the Gore family assembled each Christmas at the senior Gores' farm home in Carthage, a small town sixty miles east of Nashville.

Al and Tipper Gore brought their four children home to Tennessee in December 1986, to the elder Gores' farm, where the children clamored for a dinner that only Mattie Lucy Payne, the Gores' cook for four decades, could prepare.

After a meal of "Mattie's fried chicken," cheese potatoes, green beans, squash, fried corn, salad with watercress, cornbread, and chocolate cake, the elder Gore conferred with his senator son in the paneled library of the Gore home. Wasting no time on Senate gossip or farm business, the elder Gore shocked his son as he told him he felt the Democratic Party would turn to him as its nominee in 1988.

The gray-haired former senator lowered his voice and moved closer to his son, then told him his theory of how American people compensate for the inadequacies of a presidency by selecting its antithesis, citing Eisenhower's second term and John Kennedy, then Jimmy Carter after Nixon. [2]

Comparing his son with Jack Kennedy, who was the youngest president in history and who replaced the nation's oldest at that time, he reminded young Gore that the South was the key to the next election, that neither party in the last 20 years had been able to elect its ticket without carrying the South.

After there was no rebuttal, they rejoined the family, where Mattie was parceling out huge chunks of her moist chocolate cake. There was no more discussion of the issue that evening at the Gore home, as the talk drifted from Mattie's excellent dinner to the children's activities and interests.

Following their return to the political scene in Washington, pressure mounted for Gore to make a run for the nomination. Concerned that a lengthy campaign might affect their marriage and their children, Al and Tipper began a series of lengthy serious conversations. "I told him it was shock therapy," Tipper said in a recent interview. "I was just beginning a tour to promote my book at the time, and we were concerned about the children," she recalled. [3]

"I was upset that he would even consider it [the race] at this time. His timing was atrocious. He was starting well after the other candidates, and I was already away from home a great deal." [4] (Tipper's book, *Raising PG Kids in an X-Rated Society,* had just begun selling well, primarily to parents concerned about the effect of sex-saturated and violence-oriented rock music albums and videos on their teenage children.)

"I told him that I had already given up a job as a photo-journalist at *The Tennessean*, something I liked and was good at, so that he could begin his political career. I was doing very well when I gave that up, and I wondered if that wasn't enough." [5]

In spite of her frustration, she agreed to support him if he decided to enter the race. Gore had one more obstacle, and that was to determine his children's reaction to his candidacy.

There was no serious objection at the family conference which followed. Al III, however, asked his father, "Can't you at least wait until I'm five?" Eight-year-old Sarah expressed her concern about Secret Service protection: "When is Social Security going to start following us around?"[6]

Unknown even to his father or Tipper, Gore began asking trusted friends and colleagues about the race, soliciting their views as to the timing and his chances. Aware that his attorney parents had years of

Al Gore family (left to right): Kristin, Al, Albert III, Karenna, Tipper, and Sarah.

high level political experience, Gore decided he would seek their input on the most important decision of his political career: "Should I run for the presidency of the United States?"

He wondered, as he approached their Capitol Hill apartment, how many parents had been approached by one of their children with a question of that import.

Robert Sherborne, writing for Nashville's morning newspaper, *The Tennessean*,[7] reported on Gore's meeting with his parents:

At 9:00 A.M., Thursday, April 9, 1987, Al walked through the front door of the Methodist House on Capitol Hill, still undecided whether to make the race, eager to get his parents', particularly his father's, advice. Former Senator Gore and Pauline Gore knew he was coming, and knew the problem he was facing.

"We spent more than two hours together talking," said the elder Gore. "We tried to look at the situation factually, if the word factually can be applied to a political situation."

"We went through the pros and cons thoroughly. We tried to make an objective analysis."

Pauline sat nearby, listening intently. Occasionally, but not often, she interrupted the two men, and when she did, they listened intently. They knew the experience and expertise she had in such matters, after helping her husband through ten successful campaigns for the U.S. House and Senate and helping her son through three successful campaigns for the House and one for the Senate.

But as the conversation entered the third hour, no decision had been reached.

As the analysis continued, the senior Gore became more and more convinced his son should enter the presidential race. Albert Gore made no attempt to disguise his position that he felt Al should make the attempt, and pointed out that 1988 was the right time.

"Al has the makings of a president," he said. "He is the most exciting, charismatic candidate in the race, and he has an unusual combination of a down-to-earth personality and a keen intellect. He also has a wonderful sense of humor."

"Al will be the most effective campaigner among the candidates. He has all the personal qualities which make him ideal for uniting the Democratic Party."

The former senator pointed out the changes occurring around the country that made a generational change possible in 1988, pointing out that in 1960 he saw his former colleague in the Senate, John F. Kennedy, 43, replace Dwight Eisenhower at age 70, and noted that the country was ready for that kind of change in 1988.

"Dwight Eisenhower was a good man, an honest man, but he took it kind of easy the last two years in office. When Kennedy ran to succeed him, there were very few members of the Senate who were favorable to his nomination. But Kennedy promised to 'get the country moving again,' and he was successful. And I think the sentiment for a generational change of leadership is stronger now than it was then."

As they talked, Al hit upon the negatives, pointing out the important work still remaining for him in the Senate, his obligations to their children, finances, the rigors of a campaign, and Tipper's current book promotion.

Pauline Gore took notes.

They finally ended their talk around 11:30.

"I haven't decided yet," he told his parents. "I want one more night to sleep on it."

Pauline and Albert Gore felt he had decided against making the race when he left their apartment.

As he and Tipper again discussed whether he should try or not, he decided he would look in on the children, to study their faces as he pondered his decision. He was troubled as he went from one bedroom to another, observing his children in peaceful sleep, unaware their father was in the process of making a decision that would affect their lives forever. The campaign, if he decided to make the run, would take him from his family, leaving little time for the movie they usually attended each month or the "Cosby Show" they enjoyed together on television or visiting art museums and galleries together or taking in a Bruce Springsteen or George Strait concert.

Gore has said that he thought about a great many things as he watched his children that night. He thought about the young delegates he had spoken to at Girls' State in Murfreesboro, Tennessee, several years back, and how many of them had raised their hands when he asked whether they thought there would be a nuclear war in their lifetime. "I can make a contribution," he heard himself saying, "and I need to do it." His eyes filled with tears as he thought of how much time a campaign would take him from his own children, and of how precious they were to him.

He did not make his final decision until well into the next morning.

*   *   *

In the meantime, his father returned to the farm in Carthage, where he received a telephone call from Pauline. She said Al had called her but did not tell her how he had decided. He asked his mother, however, if she would pick his children up at their respective schools and "get them into good clothes."

At about 11:00 A.M. on April 10, 1987, Al called his father. "Dad, the word is go. I'm going for the nomination."

Young Gore had barely finished saying that he was making the race when he heard a tremendous Indianlike yell coming through the receiver. The senior Gore has said that when he heard Al say he was running, "I couldn't contain myself. I yelled like a Comanche. Then I congratulated him on his decision, and offered to help any way I could."

When Pauline Gore was asked why Al had agonized over the decision, she said, "I think my son had to establish that it would be his campaign, and that he'd be doing it in his own way."[8]

Throughout the decision process, he sought the advice of his closest friends in the Congress, Senator Jim Sasser and Representatives Bart Gordon and Jim Cooper, members of the Tennessee legislative delegation. After the legislative trio urged him to run and pledged full support, Senator Sasser volunteered to handle arrangements for the announcement.

Sasser, a highly respected Nashville lawyer, had become close to the Gore family in 1970 when he was Davidson County manager of the elder Gore's last political campaign. Sasser had another tie to the Gore family: his wife, Mary Gorman Sasser, was a close friend of Gore's sister, Nancy, when they attended Vanderbilt together, and she had remained

Albert and Pauline Gore

close to Nancy until Nancy's death in 1984. In addition, Al Gore genuinely liked and respected the senior senator from Tennessee.

Mike Pigott, the highly capable senior political writer for the *Nashville Banner*, [9] was in Washington for Gore's announcement around noon on April 10 at the Senate Caucus Room. He recalls a room packed with staff employees from Gore's office, Sasser's office and the offices of the representatives, as well as press and television people. From an interview with Pigott and his piece in the April 11, 1987 *Nashville Banner*, the announcement story continues.

"Tipper Gore was outstandingly attractive that day," he said, "and dressed in a bright red outfit." Pauline Gore, he recalled, was attractively dressed but in much more muted tones than Tipper.[10]

A newspaper article reported that the Gore family looked as if "they should have been on the cover of "Family Life.""[11]

Understandably excited about the historic event their father was involved in, the children were nevertheless concerned about why their grandfather, Albert Gore Sr., was not at the Senate Caucus Room when they arrived. He was, they were told, back in Tennessee substituting for their father at a speaking engagement in Jackson.

In addition to the announcement of the morning, the press also learned that there would be a formal opening ceremony for the Gore campaign

Jim Sasser

Mary Sasser

probably on the steps of the Smith County Courthouse later in the summer.

After he had welcomed the press and TV representatives, Senator Sasser recognized members of the Gore family and Representatives Gordon and Cooper. "I have pledged to help Al Gore any way I can," said Sasser, looking at his youthful colleague. "He has the qualities of leadership that America needs, and I'm proud to be his friend."

"I present my friend, my colleague, the next president of the United States, Senator Albert Gore Jr. of Tennessee."

As applause broke out, Gore, handsomely attired in a conservative blue suit and red tie, stepped to the podium that was positioned in front of the fireplace under a portrait of George Washington, waved to friends in the press corps, then after a quick glance at his family, spoke forcefully and confidently to the reporters who had crowded into the packed room. There were frequent bursts of applause.

"It is time for our country to turn to youth, vigor, intellectual capacity and a determination to face the problems of the future with vigor and energy," he said.

In his press conference which followed, Gore stressed that he was a national candidate, not just a "regional" candidate aiming at the fourteen Southern "Super Tuesday" primaries March 8th. "I will not be running as a regional candidate," he said. "I intend to campaign vigorously in every part of our country."

Jim Cooper   Bart Gordon

When a reporter misstated his age as thirty-eight, Gore quipped: "If I were only thirty-eight years old, I wouldn't even consider this." He noted that most of the drafters of the Constitution had been younger than he was now, and that they had set the minimum age for a president at "thirty-five, not forty-five, and there was a reason." Gore said that fifty-eight percent of the voters in 1988 would be under forty and younger than he. He noted also that the election of 1988 would mark the first time the entire "baby boomer" generation would be able to vote, and that the next president would be the last with the opportunity to serve an eight-year term in the twentieth century.

Gore confided to reporters that he was running four miles each morning to stay fit for the grueling schedule of a presidential campaign.

At forty, Gore would be the youngest person ever elected to the presidency. The youngest person ever nominated for the position was William Jennings Bryan, at thirty-six, in 1900.

After being advised that Gore had officially announced, Governor Ned McWherter of Tennessee said, "Tennessee is fortunate to have a favorite son with the intelligence and integrity of Senator Albert Gore. I want to be the first to endorse his candidacy for the presidency, and also the first to contribute to his campaign." McWherter then produced a $1,000 check with Gore's name on it.

The Tennessean and *The Nashville Banner*, morning and afternoon papers in Nashville, led an unprecedented number of Tennessee newspapers in their endorsement of Gore's presidential try, citing his leadership ability, his integrity and his intellectual capacity. A chain of seven newspapers editorialized that " without question he possesses the qualities and attributes to make him a successful national and world leader. . . . He dons the clothes of honesty and integrity. He places family atop his agenda of priorities. He beams intelligence, compassion and concern."

*   *   *

In the wake of the outpouring of support from his friends in Tennessee, Gore began his campaign in earnest. But between strategy meetings and telephone calls to political leaders and campaign contributors, he interrupted his activities to fly to the Soviet Union to speak to the International Physicians for the Prevention of Nuclear War, an internationally known and respected organization, winner of the Nobel Peace Prize in 1985. The organization is made up of 150,000 doctors from all parts of the world.

In addressing the opening session of their Seventh World Congress in Moscow, Gore honored a long-standing commitment.

Anatoly Dobrynin, formerly ambassador to the United States and now secretary of the Central Committee of the Soviet Communist Party, read the delegates a speech by Secretary Mikhail Gorbachev, then Gore spoke to the approximately two thousand physician-delegates, including five hundred from the Soviet Union.

Gore told them that the U.S. Senate would welcome the opportunity to ratify a good, comprehensive, verifiable treaty in 1988.

He outlined his plan for preventing nuclear war between the United States and the Soviet Union, stating that a verifiable arms-control agreement would make it impossible for either side to mass forces secretly near East-West borders. This, he told the prestigious congress, would reduce the fear of a conventional attack and would become a key element in producing a stable peace. He said that American fear of a Soviet strike has led to President Reagan's proposed space-based missile defense system called the Strategic Defense Initiative, which in turn has inspired fear among the Soviets.

"We must be doctors to each other's fears," he said, "and seek to dispel them by removing any rational basis for them."

Al Gore III and his father Al Gore Jr. (1987)

Albert Gore Sr. campaigns for reelection to the House (Oct. 1944)

Chapter Two

Wednesday, March 31, 1948.

Soviet armed forces in Germany refused to allow an American train to pass through the Russian zone. This action created a military and diplomatic crisis for the United States.

President Truman signed into law a housing bill that provided two billion dollars to insure home mortgages.

General of the Army Douglas MacArthur announced his willingness to accept the presidential nomination of the Republican Party, if offered.

Former Vice-President Henry A. Wallace was booed with cries of "Down with Russia—down with communism" when he brought his Third Party presidential campaign to Brooklyn.

Closer to Al Gore Jr's Tennessee home in Carthage, a Rickman youth was treated in a Livingston, Tennessee, hospital, after he had lost three fingers in a power saw accident.

Television was still in its infancy, but the air crackled that day as radio stations reported on General MacArthur's political aspirations and former Vice-President Wallace's treatment in Brooklyn. The accident involving the Tennessee youth even made the newspapers in Nashville, seventy-five miles away. A Soviet blockade in Berlin that threatened world peace, or the two billion dollar housing bill he had voted for in Congress, might normally have interested U.S. Representative Albert Gore Sr., but on March 31, 1948, the Tennessee congressman had a far more pressing matter to attend to—the birth of his son.

The Congressman was in his fifth term of Congress in 1948, elected to represent constituents in the Fourth Congressional District of Tennessee, mainly rural counties that surrounded his home county of Smith. Gore had grown up in Smith County and was well known in Carthage, its seat, a small town sixty miles east of Nashville.

Al Gore   The Fairfax, Washington, D.C.

He was a handsome man, intelligent, and had worked hard to win his district's seat in Congress, which in the shank of the Depression '30's paid a substantial yearly salary of $7,500. Tennessee received the best side of the trade, because he and Pauline, his wife, went to Washington as a team; both worked in his congressional office. Albert Gore Sr. wanted her help because he knew the scope of her intelligence and trusted her judgment and great political instincts. So that she would be able to handle almost full-time social and work responsibilities, they brought a nurse from Tennessee, Mrs. Ocie Bell, to care for Nancy, their daughter.

Representative Gore made no secret that he wanted their second child to be a boy, and he had even discussed his preference with news reporters.

In 1948 the Gores lived in Arlington, Virginia, where they had moved from Carthage after his first election to Congress in 1938. A moderate and frugal couple who had weathered bad financial times, they had first rented an apartment in Arlington Village for $62.50 per month, and the house they had rented later was only slightly more expensive.

Although Representative Gore realized that purchasing a residence in the Washington area would be a smarter financial move, he had insisted that they rent. He had a hard and fast rule that as long as they represented the voters of Tennessee, they would never buy a home anywhere else. Home was Smith County, and the farm country around Carthage, and there was to be no deviation from this rule.

After an extensive investigation for a facility that provided outstanding obstetrical care, the couple had selected Columbia Hospital for the birth of their second child. In northwest Washington at 2425 L Street, Columbia Hospital for Women was easily accessible from either the Gore residence in Arlington or his Capitol Hill office.

Nancy, 10, stayed with their housekeeper when Representative Gore drove Pauline to the hospital and admitted her. Not long thereafter Pauline Gore, 36, gave birth to their second child, a beautiful and healthy 9 pound, 2 ounce, son. Albert Arnold Gore Jr. seemed the only appropriate name.

After a flurry of telephone calls to his office and congressional associates and colleagues, the proud father notified friends and neighbors in Arlington and back home in Tennessee. Moments later he discovered that he had overlooked another call, one he considered of the highest urgency. After the call was made, the following article appeared on the front page of the next day's edition of *The Nashville Tennessean*. Headlined "Well, Mr. Gore, Here He Is—On Page 1," it read:

April 1. "From Washington Bureau WASHINGTON—A son was born to Mrs. Pauline Gore in Washington yesterday and *The Nashville Tennessean* hereby makes good on a long-standing promise to Rep. Albert Gore to give this good news page 1 play.

"The fourth district congressman extracted the promise from *The Tennessean's* Washington bureau several months ago at the time of the birth of a girl baby to Rep. and Mrs. Estes Kefauver, of Chattanooga.

"*The Tennessean* ran the Kefauver baby story on an inside page. Which led Representative Gore to comment:

"'If I have a boy baby, I don't want the news buried in the inside of the paper. I want it on page 1 where it belongs.'"

"The baby weighed 9 pounds, 2 ounces, and is doing fine. So is Mrs. Gore. They are at Columbia Hospital."

"The Gores' other child, 10-year-old Nancy, was at home calling up everybody in the telephone directory."[1]

* * *

Had the newly born infant been allowed to select his own parents, he could not have found more intelligent, energetic and goal-oriented parents than Albert and Pauline Gore. Both born in rural Tennessee farm communities, they had overcome tremendous obstacles to secure undergraduate and law degrees, and to make contacts through the years that brought them to Washington, D.C.

Albert Gore Sr. was born on December 26, 1907, to Allen and Maggie

Pauline, Al, and Albert Gore (Photo courtesy *The Nashville Banner*)

Denney Gore in Granville, a small community near Carthage that rests in the midst of the rugged, hilly terrain of Jackson County, Tennessee.

His father, Allen Gore, a farmer most of his life, was born on May 20, 1869. His family could trace its ancestry back to a Gore who fought against the British during the Revolutionary War and later received a land grant in Overton County, Tennessee. Allen Gore's father was Claiborn C. Gore, an Overton County farmer born January 16, 1840, who married Elizabeth Robinson, daughter of Allen Robinson and Martha Stanford. [2]

Allen Gore died on March 3, 1956, and was buried in Ridgewood Cemetery near Carthage. His wife, Maggie, was a daughter of Brown and Betty Waggoner Denney and a member of the Carthage Missionary Baptist Church. After her death at 84 on July 10, 1963, she too was buried at Ridgewood Cemetery. A favorite of his grandparents, young Al Gore Jr. took their deaths "very hard," according to sources who knew young Gore well during that period.

When Albert Sr. was very young, his parents moved the family to a small farm in the Grant community in neighboring Smith County. It was here that Albert Sr. grew up.

After attending college for several years on a part-time and irregular basis while he worked as a truck driver, farmer, teacher, and feed mill operator, Gore finally received his bachelor's degree from Murfreesboro Teacher's College [now Middle Tennessee State University] in 1933. After teaching and serving as a rural school principal, he was elected superintendent of Smith County Schools.

An outstanding baseball player in his youth, he also became a "pretty good fiddler" and played for square dances and at family and neighborhood gatherings. This proficiency made him popular and sought-after among relatives and neighbors in the county. When he saw that his musical skill made him attractive to voters, he used it in early elections. But after Pauline told him that she disapproved of his fiddle playing during campaigns, considering it somewhat undignified, he abandoned the practice. [3]

His earliest statewide political activities came when he managed two unsuccessful campaigns by Gordon Browning for the U.S. Senate. After Gordon Browning was elected governor of Tennessee in 1936, one of his first appointments in 1937 was Al Gore Sr. as Commissioner of Labor. Other reasons made 1937 an important year in Gore Sr.'s life. In addition to his appointment, he received his LLB that year from the Nashville YMCA Law School, and he married Pauline LaFon in her hometown of Jackson, Tennessee.

*   *   *

Pauline LaFon Gore grew up in a farm community near Palmersville in Weakley County, where her parents, Walter L. and Maude LaFon, had moved in 1911 from Brookland, Arkansas. Pauline was born the next year, 1912, and grew up with sisters Thelma and Verlie and brothers Gilbert, Everette and Whit (now a judge in Jackson, Tennessee).

As there was no electricity or school buses in those days, Pauline walked the two miles each day to a rural school, which required students in grades one through ten to study Latin.

Pauline played basketball in black "sateen bloomers" and wore old dresses when she waded the creek, because proper young ladies did not wear bathing suits then. Pauline's life was centered in her family, her school and the rural Church (of Christ) the family attended.

In 1925 Walter and Maude moved the LaFon family on a farm wagon to nearby Jackson, where Pauline was an outstanding high school student. After her graduation from Union University at Jackson, her father encouraged her to attend Vanderbilt University Law School, where she became the second female student in its history.

While she was a student at Vanderbilt, she lived at the Nashville YMCA to save money. She took a job around the corner at the Andrew Jackson Hotel coffee shop, waiting tables from 5:30 to 10:00 each night,

Maggie Denney Gore and Allen Gore (1952)

and it was there that the tall, attractive law student with brown hair and blue eyes met another aspiring law student.

Pauline Gore told *The Nashville Tennessean* in 1970 about her courtship by Al Gore Sr., then a twenty-eight-year-old Smith County School superintendent, who attended night law school at the nearby YMCA and came by three nights a week before driving back to Carthage:

"He would come into the coffee shop for coffee to keep awake driving home. He was a friend of Gordon Browning [who later became Tennessee governor] whose secretary was from my home town. I guess that's who introduced us. There was actually no dramatic moment when we met, as I recall. I was just suddenly aware of this handsome young man coming in for coffee. We started dating. He was very serious even then. I couldn't tempt him to leave any serious work, no matter how fancy a party we were invited to. That was what bothered me most at that age."[4]

After she received her law degree from Vanderbilt, she practiced law for a year in Texarkana, Arkansas. Following her marriage to Albert Gore on April 17, 1937, she withdrew from active law practice and devoted herself to his career and their home and marriage. In 1957 she was interviewed by Louise Davis of *The Nashville Tennessean*, who provided this glimpse of the life of a United States senator's wife in Washington:

"When Senator Gore was in the House, Mrs. Gore used to go to the office with him 'a good part of the time' to help relieve him of time-consuming tasks. She still pitches in on extra office duties, campaigns with him, finds immeasurable ways of helping his secretarial staff answer questions that would otherwise consume the senator's time.

"Often she meets him at the office at lunch time to entertain friends in the damask-and-chandeliered senate dining room. But more often she is attending one of the endless luncheons that whisk the wives of Washington officials from club house to hotel dining room at a dizzying pace.

"She has just finished a two-year term of office as program chairman for the Congressional Club—a purely social, non-political organization made up of wives and daughters of the members and former members of the House, and wives and daughters of justices and cabinet members. . . .

"Mrs. Gore was program chairman. . .of the Democratic Congressional Wives Forum. . .also has a special interest in the Home for the Blind in Washington.

"She makes numerous radio and television appearances, sometimes substitutes for her husband when he is unable to make a speaking appointment. She attends garden parties in the summer, teas, receptions, cocktail parties the year round."[5]

* * *

In 1938, the year in which Gore was elected to the House of Representatives from the Fourth Congressional District, the couple's first child, Nancy LaFon Gore, was born. She took her first steps in Virginia, where the Gores had stopped overnight on their way to Washington for Representative Gore to take his seat in Congress.

After attending David Lipscomb High School in Nashville one year, Nancy went on to graduate from Mount Vernon School. She later graduated from Vanderbilt University. Very idealistic, highly intelligent and well read, she pursued her idealism by volunteering for the Peace Corps, which she helped establish in the early 1960's after a meeting she and her father had with President Kennedy. After that she took a position with the United Nations Pavilion in Brussels, then returned to Tennessee to farm with her father and manage several of his state campaigns.

Though strong-willed, she was an exceptionally talented and compassionate person. The family cook said, "She liked to be out front." It was said of her that she loved everyone, regardless of their economic

Pauline, Albert, Nancy, Frank Hunger, Tipper, and Al Gore Jr. (Photo
courtesy *The Nashville Banner*)

or social status. Her fondness for animals and the land prompted her
to enter the cattle business with her father at the Gore farm.

An excellent cook, she delighted in preparing meals for her brother,
who in those days appreciated foods that would not find their way into
his diet today. In 1966 she married Greenville, Mississippi, attorney
Frank Hunger in a wedding ceremony at the Gore farm.

Nancy, a heavy smoker, was stricken with lung cancer in the midst
of her brother's 1984 Senate campaign and died at Vanderbilt Hospital
in Nashville in July of that year. He spent every spare moment that
he could with her at the hospital and was with her in her final lucid
moments. Many feel that her death had a heavy impact on his life, that
his compelling interest in environmental and health issues was in part
prompted by her tragic death. Certainly she was one of the most
important women in his life—in his younger years a caring second
mother; later, a confidante and friend. To Al and his teenage friends
in Carthage, she was important because, as they fondly recall, they could
talk with her and "feel like she could understand what we were saying."

Tipper Gore has said of their relationship: "Al took her passing very
hard....They adored each other....She was a terribly important part

Al, Albert, and Pauline Gore (1958) (Photo courtesy *The Nashville Banner*)

of Al's life. She was mediator, advisor, powerful supporter, and loving critic."[6]

*   *   *

When Representative and Mrs. Gore went to Washington, they considered themselves not only partners in marriage but a political team. They felt they should represent not only their constituents in the Fourth District but all of Tennessee as they sought to help the "small man" during the days of President Franklin D. Roosevelt's New Deal.

They, like many other Tennesseans of the time, felt a personal debt of gratitude toward President Roosevelt, and they went to Washington with a genuine desire to make a contribution toward improving their country. There was a feeling among rural people in Tennessee that FDR had personally intervened on their behalf to get electrical service to their homes and farms with his Rural Electrification Program. As they drove their livestock or farm produce to market on country roads that would be considered substandard today, or sent their children to schools built with government funds, the farm people of Tennessee offered prayers of thanks for FDR's road and WPA projects.

When Representative Albert Gore took his seat in Congress, he

Cordell Hull

Franklin D. Roosevelt Harry S. Truman

assumed a post that at one time had been held by a then current trusted adviser to President Roosevelt, Secretary of State Cordell Hull. As they were both ardent Roosevelt supporters, it was important that Secretary Hull correctly inform their constituents back in Middle Tennessee that Congressman Gore was living up to New Deal expectations. Further, Gore Sr. genuinely admired Secretary Hull and sought his counsel.

In the six years before President Roosevelt's death in 1945, Representative and Mrs. Gore consistently proved their loyalty to Roosevelt through a number of New Deal programs that helped their friends and neighbors in the rural Fourth Congressional District.

In the years that followed, in both the House and the Senate, Gore Sr. became famous for his outspoken personality, independence in thought and action, hard work, tedious preparation and a "common sense" approach to problems. He felt a need to represent constituents who had the least ability to understand their own need for representation. He served with distinction during the administrations of Roosevelt, Truman, Eisenhower, Kennedy, Johnson and Nixon. While he felt that the government should protect its citizens in a compassionate manner, he also felt that average citizens had a responsibility to do their part to make government work.

Gore Sr. remained in the House fourteen years, then in 1952 opposed an aging and popular incumbent, Senator Kenneth McKellar of Memphis. After a bitter struggle, Gore was elected and went on to represent Tennessee in the U.S. Senate for the next eighteen years.

Nancy, Pauline, Albert, and Al (1952)

Much of his success as a legislator resulted from extensive reading, strict preparation and study for debate, which was much more important in those days than it is now. Following President Roosevelt's lead, he prepared radio reports for stations in Middle Tennessee that kept listeners advised on current happenings in the Congress.

After he tired of a roadway system that required two days' drive between Carthage and Washington, he studied for, prepared and authored the Interstate Highway Act, legislation which has impacted American life as much as any of this century.

Throughout his career, the senior Gore championed the "small man" of America. His legislation helped the family farmer, the small businessman and the workingman. Though relatively unfamiliar with banking practices and economic theories when he arrived in Congress, he studied until he became an expert, generally always opposing interest hikes and the big utility interests' monopoly on energy and power.

Gore Sr. seemed to possess an uncanny ability to see where the country was moving in relation to other countries of the world. Long before President Nixon began his open-door policy with the People's Republic of China, Gore had urged recognition of that government.

In one of his books he has related a poignant story of racial discrimination, an event which caused him to become one of the first

Southern politicians to vote for measures to improve the rights of blacks. In 1956, he refused to sign the pro-segregation Southern Manifesto which South Carolina Senator Strom Thurmond had placed on his desk and insisted that he sign. He voted against the Civil Rights Act of 1964, however, and he has always said that he regretted making this vote.

His last political campaign, in 1970, was bitter throughout. His Republican opponent, Bill Brock of Chattanooga, said Gore was "out of touch with the voters of Tennessee" and "too liberal for Tennessee." On November 4, 1979, Tennessee voters turned their senior senator out of office, giving Gore 46,344 fewer votes than Brock. The truth of the matter was that Senator Gore lost to Brock because of Gore's long opposition to the Vietnam War, a position Brock referred to throughout the campaign, causing voters in Tennessee to wonder whether Gore had pulled away from the mainstream of Tennessee. In the end, however, Senator Gore's view of the Vietnam War was validated, determined to be the wise one.

When Senator Gore Sr. left the Senate in January 1971, Senate Majority Whip Edward Kennedy in a farewell tribute ranked him with "the giants" of the Senate's history, Webster, Calhoun and Clay. Kennedy said that Gore "had graced the United States Senate with his extraordinary gifts of intelligence, eloquence and wit. . . . If we see more clearly today on any of dozens of difficult issues, it is because we stand on the shoulders of giants like Albert Gore."[7]

Although hurt deeply when Tennessee voters did not return him to the Senate in 1970, Senator Albert Gore Sr. continued an active life style. He wrote a second book, lectured at colleges and universities, and during the Carter administration was named to serve with former Pennsylvania Governor William Scranton and former CIA executive Tom Farmer on a three-member Intelligence Oversight Committee.

He and Pauline practiced law with a firm in Nashville for a time, then formed a law firm in Washington. After operating their law practice several months, they established a new firm, and a branch was created in Los Angeles.

One of their firm's clients, Island Creek Coal Company of Cleveland, Ohio, recruited Senator Gore to become their full-time chairman of the board and a director and vice-president of Occidental Petroleum Company. He accepted and moved his corporate headquarters to Lexington, Kentucky.

Pauline remained a member of the law firm, but after a time, Albert Sr.'s duties required so much travel throughout the world that she retired from practice to travel with him and assist in his new career. He retired several years later, devoting his primary energies to assisting his son and fulfilling his duties as a grandfather.

Albert, Al, and Pauline Gore (1970)

Albert Gore Sr. is now a distinguished eighty, but he looks and acts much younger and resembles Hollywood's version of what a senator should look like. White haired and quick witted, he provides advice when Al Jr. asks for it, but does not interfere with his son's political life, stating that his son is his own man.

Gore Sr. and Pauline gave up their apartment at the Fairfax in 1968. They now live in an apartment on Capitol Hill within walking distance of the Capitol, the Senate office buildings and the House buildings.

During the Democratic Party presidential campaign, Mr. and Mrs. Gore Sr. spent a great deal of their time supporting their son's effort. "The best thing Mrs. Gore and I can do to help Al and Tipper in their try for the White House," he said, "is to give them the knowledge that their four children are safe and being well cared for."

The senior Gore said recently, "You can put this on the record. Al has the personal characteristics and the attributes of character required for national leadership. But whether the lightning will ever strike, only fate and the future will tell."[8]

Jack Robinson, a highly respected Nashville attorney and a former law partner of the Gores, grew up in Carthage, where he knew the Gore family as neighbors and friends. A graduate of both the University of Tennessee and George Washington University Law School, Robinson worked as administrative assistant to the senior Gore in his Senate office from December 1956 until 1964.

"Albert Sr. is one of the finest, most straightforward and honest men I've known in my lifetime," said Robinson. "I've seen him do the right thing time after time, even when he knew that doing it would hurt him politically. . . . He was ahead of his time in honesty and telling the American people the truth."

"I got to know his family well when I worked for the Senator," Robinson continued. "Pauline, his wife, is an outstanding attorney in her own right. . . . I also saw young Al Gore Jr. a lot then, and we've stayed in touch since. What is difficult for me to understand is why America is taking so long to see what a treasure they finally have in Al Gore Jr. He's a serious-minded young man, always well prepared, very sensitive, and has honesty, depth of character,intelligence, everything it takes to be a good and effective public servant. . . . Al Jr's always been competitive, was a competitive young man then, in his eighth to fifteenth years. He constantly pushed himself to excel in academics and sports."

"During the time I worked for his father," Robinson recalled, "the family lived in an apartment on the eighth floor of the Fairfax Hotel at 2100 Massachusetts Avenue. The Fairfax has been renovated since the Gores lived there. It's fairly luxurious now, but it was rather plain then. No paneling to speak of, certainly not the 'posh' place it's been characterized as in press and TV reports I've seen about young Al."

"Al is like his father. Always considered Carthage as home, and Smith County folks know the whole family," Robinson said. "You can't fool hill people, and that's what Carthage folks are. They're the best indicators as to Al—gave him almost 100% of the entire vote in every election."

"I remember how hard the boy has always worked in tobacco and the calves he'd raise for 4-H projects," Robinson concluded. "I've seen the worst and the best in politics. . . and he's the best."

Albert Gore Sr. and Pauline Gore (1970; photo by Jack Gunter, courtesy *Nashville Banner*)

Nancy Gore Hunger (photo courtesy *Nashville Banner*)

Chapter Three

As much as I converse with sages and heroes, they have very little of my love and admiration. I long for rural and domestic scenes, for the warbling of birds and the prattling of my children.

John Adams

Al, Albert Sr., and Pauline Gore (1958; photo courtesy of *The Nashville Banner*)

Albert Sr. and Al Gore Jr.

Al Gore was the product of two locations, two homes, two societies, two life styles, two families, but he says his upbringing in both urban and rural settings gave him an insight for which he's grateful. On any given day, he might have listened to his father, an important U.S. Senator, discuss racial conditions in the South with John F. Kennedy, or chopped row after row of corn with Gordon Thompson in a Caney Fork River bottom field.

His life was divided both emotionally and geographically between the eighth floor of a downtown Washington hotel and a 250-acre farm in Carthage, a town of 2,500 just 60 miles due east of Nashville.

"I've always had two separate lives," Gore told Nolan Walters of Knight-Ridder newspapers. "My parents had two homes, an apartment in Washington and a farm in Tennessee. I went to the public school in Carthage in Tennessee and St. Albans in Washington, and have friends in both places. I attend a church when I'm in Tennessee and another in Arlington. I am what I am. . . . I grew up on a farm, I know farm life and I am a farmer. . . but I'm happy that my parents gave me a good education. . . but if you're a boy, and you have the choice between the eighth floor of a hotel and a big farm with horses, cows, canoes and a river, it was an easy choice for me."[1]

The farm Gore speaks so nostalgically about is about 2 1/2 miles east

Alota and William Thompson

of downtown Carthage on Highway 70N, which used to be the principal connector between Nashville and Knoxville in the days before Senator Gore Sr. built the interstate highway system that gave Tennessee Interstate 40. Just west of the Benton McMillan Memorial Bridge and the river it spans, the Caney Fork, there is a huge sign in the shape of a cow that reads, "GORE FARMS."

The house on the Gore place is on the bluff that overlooks the bridge and the river. Though not extravagant by today's standards, it was the finest home in Smith County when it was completed in 1961 or 1962. In the years that preceded its building, the Gores owned several houses in and around downtown Carthage. Al and Tipper have a farm and home across the river.

Al Gore was five when Alota Thompson and her husband, William, moved into the old tenant house on Senator Albert Gore's farm in Elmwood, where they would live and care for the crops and livestock. From the day they moved to the farm in 1953 until they left in 1962, during each summer, congressional recess and vacation period and during his entire seventh year, Gore lived with William and Alota Thompson, whom Gore even now calls his "second mother."

After meeting the Thompsons, it's easy to understand Gore's affection for them. William Thompson, neatly dressed in a red and black plaid shirt and freshly pressed bib overalls, and his attractive wife Alota, attired in stylish black slacks and a red blouse, were hospitable, open, and eager to discuss "their second son."

"He was such a good little boy," they both said, and "anything we did in helping raise him was our good fortune, because we loved him like our own boy, Gordon, who grew up like Al's brother."

The Thompsons are still devoted to the elder Gores, whom they admire. They attended a school where "the Senator" taught years ago. "Senator and Mrs. Gore are fine people, and were awfully busy when Al was a little boy," they both said, noting that young Al was only four when his father was first elected to the Senate.

"When Al was a little boy, he would fall asleep and we couldn't get him to wake up," Mr. Thompson said. "I would carry him in and put him on the bed and take his clothes off."

Alota interjected that she resented the recent stories and news reports that Al Gore Jr. had little to do with Carthage and was not a farmer. "Anyone who says Al Gore Jr. is not a farmer doesn't know the same Al Gore I know," Alota says, lovingly. "He worked right with us on the farm, he and Gordon. He went to the tobacco patch with a hoe. He loves the farm. It bothers me when they print things in the paper and in magazines that aren't true. He loves everything about the farm, riding the mules and ponies, and being out in the fields."

The attractive farm lady continued, "When we moved there, we didn't have water in the house—no bathrooms—but we hadn't lived there too long till they remodeled the house. That didn't make a bit of difference to Al. He didn't care. It didn't bother him."

Asked whether the farm people in Smith County resent young Gore's education, she replied, "No, I'm happy he got a good high school education, got to go to Harvard. I wish my boy could have, too. But all that didn't make any difference to Al. When they were having hearings on shift work in factories, Al sent for Gordon and had him testify about how hard shift work in factories was and how it affected your health. Gordon stayed at Al's folks' apartment while he and his wife were there for the hearings."

She said, "He knows how country people live and how the city people live. I think that is what helped him so much. He knows how the country people have lived and still knows."

Mr. Thompson recalled that when Al was about six, he and Gordon Thompson discovered a wasps' nest in an outhouse. They began throwing rocks at it to knock it down. Al was struck in the head with a rock and had to be taken to the hospital in Carthage. "The doctor put in several stitches," Alota said. "I believe I could find the scar today."

They said that until he got into the higher grades, Al attended the elementary school in Carthage, where Miss Eleanor Smotherman taught him one year. Miss Smotherman, according to the Thompsons, is the best-known teacher in Smith County, having taught generations of county residents. "He's the smartest child I've ever taught," she had told the Thompsons.

"When he was eight, Mr. Gore gave him a spotted pony for Christmas," Alota continued. "He loved that pony so much, and rode it all the time. The pony reared up once when Al was riding him, and rolled over on him. We were relieved when Al jumped up and said he wasn't hurt."

Mrs. Thompson pointed with considerable pride to an oil painting which adorns their living room. "That's Patsy," she said, "Gordon's little bulldog that Al loved so much. The boys made a little harness for Patsy, and she'd pull them around the yard for hours in a wagon. She disappeared for several days once. Al never wanted to give up searching for her, even when we did. We'd looked everywhere for her. I was just torn up because I loved Patsy so, and the boys knew it. I'd sit around and worry that Patsy had been stolen, or killed or lying somewhere hurt, and Al would comfort me, give me hope. He refused to let me get down, and he'd tell me, 'We'll find her, I know we will, just don't worry,' and then I'd feel better. And when we found her, after several days, alive and well, trapped in an old corncrib on the back of the place, I was so happy and so was Al."

"There were so many things he loved to do on the farm," Mr. Thompson recalled. "You'd have to know country life to appreciate this, but he enjoyed swimming in the cow trough. It would get hot and we'd find Al and Gordon jumping in that trough, filled with smelly sulphur water. He swam some, too, over at the pool at Carthage, but he said swimming in the cow trough was a lot more fun for him. He liked anything to do with physical exertion and excitement."

The Thompsons recalled that Al Gore had always attended church faithfully. "We took him with us a lot," they said, "and he and his family always go to the New Salem Baptist Church, about a mile up the road, when they come home."

But, Mr. Thompson said, the farm was more than play, and "Al worked right along with us in the fields. Senator Gore was afraid he'd grow up without learning to work, and cautioned me to keep him busy."

"I tried," he said.

"Al was never a picky eater," Alota testified. "During much of that time I worked as a nurse in Carthage and had to get up and leave early. William would get the boys up and fix breakfast. Al especially liked cinnamon toast, and William would fix that 'most every morning. At night he'd eat anything on the table, but hamburgers and vegetables were his favorites," she recalled.

Gordon Thompson

"Al Gore Jr. is so intelligent and loving. He would make a wonderful president," they both said. "His heart is so good. He loves the common man, and there's no pretense about him."

*   *   *

Gordon Thompson knew Al Gore better than anyone else in those early, formative years and considers him a close friend. Thompson works in a hot, noisy factory, but years ago he and Al Gore lived as brothers on the huge Gore farm.

"When he first started staying with us, he had been around Washington but had never lived on a farm," Thompson said. "He had to get accustomed to the people here and the way we lived. When Al first started staying with us, we didn't even have a bathroom, just an outside toilet. There was no running water in the house. I guess it was three or four years before we got it. He never complained. He never complained about nothing. He just fit in. He knows what it means to come up with not having much, especially when he stayed with us."

"He's one of the smartest and best people I've ever known," Thompson attested. "A fine man, he'll make a great president."

Thompson recalls Al as fun-loving, cheerful, always laughing. "We

Al Gore Jr. with prize Angus

had a lot of good times growing up, like making that harness for Patsy, my dog, and having her pull us around. He was always funny and joking. He liked to pull pranks. It takes a while to get to know Al. But I knew him since we were little. If you don't know him, it takes a while. He kinda comes across as a stiff shirt, but he's not."

Thompson says the thing that impresses him most about Al Gore is that once you're his friend, you're a friend for life, and he never gets "too big or too busy" for his country associates. "He don't use friends," Thompson said. "A couple years ago I was working shift work in this factory, which is pretty rough, rotating your days and nights, and working hard in there, and Al was home, and he had us down for supper at his house and I told him that it was pretty rough, working factory shift work. I didn't think anything about it until a few months later I got a call to come to testify before this committee he had on health that was studying what shift work does to your body. He took me to lunch two or three times and I got to talk to him. I really enjoyed that."

"He believes in hard work, and grew up in it," Thompson recalled. "He learned a lot about farming when we were growing up. We had to do our own cooking lots of the time. Al worked hard. His dad was pretty strict on him. He [Sr.] always told my dad if Al didn't work hard, he wanted to know about it. 'I expect him to work just as hard as anybody else.' He was strict."

"Al really lived two different life styles, had two lives," Gordon Thompson said. "One thing stands out about Al and his life in Washington. All the time he was with us, he never mentioned the first person in Washington."

"Al was home in Carthage," Thompson reflected. "He wanted to leave Washington behind."

*　　*　　*

Miss Eleanor Smotherman taught young Al Gore in the second-grade at Carthage Elementary School, not far from the Main Street home in which she grew up and has lived all her life. She's retired now, but substitutes in the county whenever she's needed, which is almost every day. It's considered a mark of excellence now in Carthage to have been in one of the fifty second-grade classes taught by Miss Smotherman, a bona fide treasure of the county.

"His intelligence was frightening," she said. "Al Gore Jr. was so mature and advanced I had to almost look at him to see whether he was a child or an adult.

"Once I gave out new second-grade readers, and told my students they could take them home to show their parents what they were reading. I told them that if they wished, they could read the first story in the book, which consisted of seven pages."

"The next morning Al was at my desk with the reader under his arm," she recalled. He said, "I've read it, Miss Smotherman.'

"'That's good, honey,' I said. 'Did you enjoy the story?'"

Gore looked her straight in the eye and said, coolly, "No, Ma'am, the whole book."

The engaging country schoolteacher looked at the small boy, bright-eyed with excitement, for a few moments, so stunned that she couldn't respond. Then she told him that she had been to college for five years where they had taught her to teach school, but no one had ever prepared her for a student like him.

"He had such drive, such enthusiasm, such intelligence, it made it a joy to have him in class," she said. "I taught in this school system back in the '30's when his father was my county superintendent, and I know that many people have the mental capability to do the work but won't push themselves to do it. Al would, just like his father."

"I have always wanted my picture made with him, but I think I embarrassed him back in 1976 when he first ran for Congress. I asked him to pose with me," she said. "I told him then that I wanted my picture made with the president of the United States, but it was never made, and probably never will be now. . . . I would consider it an honor."

Eleanor Smotherman

"Integrity. . .honor. . .honesty. . .intelligence. . .compassion—those are words that come to mind when I think of Al Gore Jr.," she said.

Miss Smotherman said that she had never before been so impressed with a politician, then changed her mind and said the word *politician* didn't seem to apply to Al Gore. She called him a "craftsman of government, the best she had ever seen, a man with executive ability."

Miss Hallie Lee Smith is another retired schoolteacher who still lives in Carthage. She recalls Al Gore Jr. as a member of her third-grade class at Carthage Elementary from September to Christmas. "His parents took him back to Washington then," she explained. "He was a bright, studious little boy, a very good reader, and very cooperative."

Miss Smith said that Al was afraid he might be treated differently from the other students, and in a rural school setting, only rarely do parents come to the classroom. One day Pauline Gore came by her room to have Al leave class early to accompany her. Obviously upset to see his mother at the school, Al put his head down on his desk and didn't come forward when his name was called. When Miss Smith asked him why he hadn't responded, he said, "Mother, the other parents don't come after their children."

Miss Smith recalled that Al was never a disciplinary problem, but one day she noticed a commotion near the front of the lunch line as

Hallie Smith

her students made their selections in the cafeteria. She went to check and found that the children behind Al were upset. He had bought every remaining roll, all nineteen of them, and put them on his tray.

"Al," she said, "why did you take so many rolls? You can't eat that many, and they cost five cents each."

"Oh, Miss Smith," the youngster replied, "I *can* eat them all, too. Maybe not all at lunch, but these are the best rolls I ever ate, and I can take those I don't eat here home with me and eat them."

Stifling a laugh in front of the children, she explained what would happen if he bought them all. Al understood and the commotion ended. "I will never forget Al and the rolls," she said.

"He'll make a fine president," she said.

*   *   *

But if the farm life sounds too idyllic, life in the Gore apartment in Washington was somewhat different. In May 1957, when little Al was nine, living at the Fairfax and going to exclusive St. Albans, Pauline Gore was interviewed by Louise Davis for the *Nashville Tennessean* article quoted earlier. Mrs. Gore said: "He [Al] likes for me to be here when he gets home from St. Albans School at 4:30 PM. Our two

Al Gore's elementary school in Carthage

bedroom apartment. . .is just right for us. . . .Our day begins at 7:00 AM, and I arrange it so those first fifty-five minutes—about the most important of the day for Albert Sr.—are for him and little Al to get in a visit together. While I prepare breakfast—pancakes are favorites— they get in a little 'rassling' and horseplay while they dress. Breakfast is leisurely, with lots of time for talk. And then Al's school car comes by to pick him up at 7:55."[2]

Pauline Gore continued: "Even though Albert and I are going out to dinner later, I cook Al's dinner and sit at the table with him to talk while he eats. There is nothing lonelier than a meal alone."[3]

The article indicated that the Gores enjoyed walking after dinner, usually out beautiful Massachusetts Avenue, past the "imposing row of embassies with exotic banners flying." They used the time to teach their children about the world's politics and geography, and played a game that would reward them when they correctly identified an embassy by the flag which flew over it.[4]

*   *   *

"I was there to see his sister, Nancy, but there he was, a competitive eleven-year-old kid brother with a ping pong paddle in his hand, so I

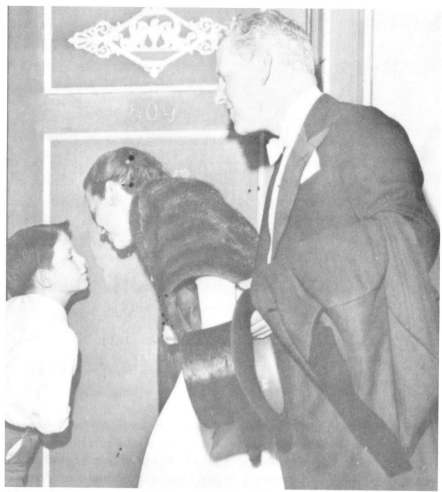

Al tells Pauline and Albert Sr. good-night before they depart for a "white tie and tails" affair at the White House. His parting remark: "Dad, save that outfit."

played ping pong," laughed Gilbert Merritt Jr., as he talked about his long friendship with the Gore family.

"I started dating Nancy during my high school days at Castle Heights," Judge Merritt said. "We continued dating during college days and remained good friends after our respective marriages. I have actually known Al Gore Jr. since he was six, and I saw him often at the Gore homes in Washington and Carthage."

"The entire Gore family is one of the most outstanding families in America, in my view", says the Sixth Circuit Court of Appeals judge, who maintains offices in Cincinnati and Nashville. "His parents are outstanding people, highly intelligent, and excellent attorneys in their

Inez Owens   Eleanor Smotherman

own right. Al Jr. inherited many of their better characteristics, and in the thirty-four years I've known him I've found that his strength is in his intellect, his character, his loyalty and preparation for leadership. He simply refuses to be ill-informed on any issue. He pushes himself mercilessly to learn and likes to compete."

Judge Merritt, formerly the federal prosecutor in Nashville, where he had a private law practice before he went on the bench, knows the pressures of leadership and the qualities of character needed to lead. During the 1960's he led the prosecution team that hunted down and prosecuted the most notorious bank robbery gang in Middle Tennessee's history.

Judge Merritt says that Al Gore represents the very best in American politics and "believes in public service of the highest calling." He said, "Al Gore has the highest ethical and personal standards I've ever seen in government service." He credits Gore's parents.

"In spite of great self-confidence, self-reliance in the best sense of the word, he is one of the kindest persons I've ever known," Merritt said. "He's in a picture-perfect marriage to one of the kindest and best women in America. In my opinion, Al Gore is the best qualified man in America for the presidency."

Another person who was very important in Al Gore Jr.'s life from the time he was twelve throughout his college years was Inez Owens, an elderly black lady who lives in an upstairs apartment at her sister's home in downtown Carthage.

"I'm not rich," she said, "but I have something so valuable to me I'll never part with it as long as I'm alive." Then she made her way in the darkened apartment to an old dresser in the corner of the room, where she says she "keeps what little I got." After several minutes of rummaging through the papers and some old pictures, she found what she had searched for.

"It's me," she said proudly. "Me in the picture with little Al, last summer when he made his speech up at the courthouse. I was there and they made my picture with him."

The picture's bright colors conflict with the darkness and drabness of the room, but it's apparent why she's so proud of the photograph. She's in the center, a proud black woman wearing a new blue dress and a white hat, fanning herself with a red, white and blue fan that has "Al Gore" emblazoned across it.

"No, I can't let it get out of my sight, even to put it in Al's book," she said, retrieving the picture. "But I'll let you make one today."

"I sewed for the Gore family from the time Al was a youngster," she said. She made draperies and slipcovers for the Gore household and patched clothing, mainly young Al's, and sewed dresses for Pauline and daughter Nancy.

"My four grandparents were all slaves," the elderly lady said. "But Al was just as proud of me. He always introduced his school friends who came down to me."

"I made him a robe once for school, and he used it. I wonder if he still has it?" she pondered.

"Oh, he was all boy, all right. He liked to play in faded blue jeans, and the more holes they had the better. He'd go all over that farm, and down that river in his little boat. . . . He liked to wear his blue jeans cut off at the knee, and he would wear them out back in the seams, and then he would ask me to put patches on the seams. Then the patch would get a hole, and he'd ask me to patch them again. I told him one day, I said, 'Albert, I'm going down to the store to get you a new pair of jeans,' and he said, 'No, no, that's the way I like them, all raggy-shaggy.'"

"He is so kind and loving, a wonderful person. He always treated me with respect. He likes the 'little people.' I think he's ready to be president, being so smart and all."

*   *   *

"Tough as nails," a true friend who'd "try anything," is how Terry Pope describes Al Gore Jr., his childhood friend who's three months older than he. Today, Pope, an Air Force veteran who enlisted in 1967, works in Hendersonville at the General Electric factory, but from the time

Left to Right: Terry Pope, "Lady," and Al Gore, Jr. (1960)

they were seven until they were thirteen, they spent a part of every day of each summer together. From 1955 to 1961 the Pope family lived on the Gore farm, where Terry's father helped care for the livestock and raised crops.

"My family lived up there on the farm six years. Al and I were pretty close while we were growing up, but when we started high school, we grew apart. We were together all summer every summer from 1955 to 1961, and I think I went to school with him some, too. I was a year behind him. I don't know whether he started early. He graduated in 1965 and I got out in 1966. I remember just briefly him going to school up there at home. We were just regular farm boys, no better or worse. I know he's a good man, the best, I'm proud to have grown up with him," attested this friend from youth.

"Al was thirteen when Flame, his pony, fell on him," Terry Pope recalled. "We were riding one day and came to a gate when something frightened Flame, who reared up on his hind legs, then fell backwards on Al. I thought he was hurt bad when Flame rolled over him, but Al got from beneath him. Flame took off running, like he was crazy, with the saddle under his belly, bucking and jumping. He went out in the middle of a pond and just laid down, scared to death. He wasn't hurt. Al was like the rest of us, tough as nails," he said.

"He had a Collie named Buff, and Al gave me one of her puppies that I named Lady. After a couple of years Lady grew up awfully pretty, so much so that when Al and I were both ten, we got into an argument about whose dog was the prettiest. We went at it pretty good and spirited," he said laughing, "and it wasn't any Senate debate either. We decided to let Mrs. Gore decide, so we took our dogs up to the house and asked her to step outside and judge them. She looked them over as Al and I said why we thought our dog was the prettiest, then she said, 'I have to say that Buff is but I know you think Lady is and she is beautiful.' After Mrs. Gore said all those nice things about Lady, we left, both happy, both thinking our dog was the prettiest. That was deadly serious business to us. Later, Al's dog, Buff, was killed after she started chasing cars. Lady died while I was away in the Air Force, sometime between 1967 and 1971."

"Al and I went to 4-H camp at Crossville in 1960 at the site of an old POW camp. Al enjoyed being in the 4-H Club and working on farm projects."

"Al was an excellent strong swimmer. After they built the swimming pool in Carthage in 1957, he and I went almost every day. Al and I would have some chores to do around the house for Mrs. Gore and at the farm. That was how we got our swimming money. Work all morning and in the afternoon she would take us to the pool. She would come back and pick us up around 5:00 or 6:00."

Although an unusually stable and well disciplined youth, he was still a boy, and occasionally tested restraints placed on him. His parents, while never strict proponents of corporal punishment, expected those in charge of him during their absence to administer discipline as the situation required. When he was ten, he received "a pretty good whipping," according to Terry.

"We were playing and working at the same time," he said. "Al and I were supposed to pull the 'down row' of corn while my dad and the other men pulled several rows alongside as the team of mules pulled the wagon slowly through the field," he said, explaining how corn is gathered. The ears of corn, still in their shucks, are removed from their stalks, then tossed into the wagon. "We began throwing kernels of shelled corn at one another, one of our favorite pastimes."

After a while, he said, Al tired of throwing one kernel at a time and let fly a handful of shelled corn, which struck Mr. Pope. He called out to Al in a serious tone to stop throwing corn and pay attention to the work at hand.

Terry Pope (1988)   Terry Pope (1963)

A few moments later Gore threw another handful, and this time most of the kernels struck Mr. Pope on the face and head. He stopped the wagon, walked over to young Gore, put him over his knee and gave him a "pretty good spanking."

His eyes brimming with tears, Al looked up at him, then said, "I'm going up to the house and tell my mother. You work for my father. She won't stand for you spanking me."

By now, all the farm hands were watching the showdown. Mr. Pope took off his hat, wiped his brow, looked at Al, who was whimpering, trying hard not to cry, then spoke slowly. "Al, I'm supposed to take care of you," he said, "and I'm going to. You know how much I think of you and your family, but you didn't mind, and you deserved what you got. Now, if you're a mind to tell your mother, let's stop this wagon right here and now and both of us will march right up there to the house and tell Mrs. Gore. It's up to you," he said.

The little boy hesitated, not wanting to lose face in front of his friend but trying hard to salvage some dignity from the event.

"I'm fine," he said. "I don't see why she needs to know." The men resumed picking corn, and the two boys resumed playing, but after that Al always waited until the adults were out of his line of fire before he threw handfuls of corn.

"I was a friend of his before we started getting interested in girls. When he did start, he never had any other girl but Donna, that I knew of.

"He wasn't afraid of anything. Once he thought Mr. Thompson's coon dog Spot had gone mad, but something had scared him real bad. He started running and howling, and Al finally ran him down before he went in the river. He was all right, he'd just gotten scared.

"At ten or eleven one of our favorite pastimes was building fortresses in the hayloft on the Gore farm. We built the best one of our entire lives when we were ten or eleven, and made a network of tunnels and big headquarters room on the center from bales of hay. The tunnels came out at strategic points above where some of the farm hands were milking cows. We laid in a good supply of shelled corn, and as they milked the cows, we threw down the kernels of corn that would sting pretty good. When they looked up to check, all they could see were bales of hay. It was hilarious fun and lasted several days until they had had all they could take. They came in force with a search and destroy mission, found our tunnel and destroyed our whole complex. We barely got out ourselves and got in big trouble because we could have been hurt."

Pope saw Gore's character develop during their years of friendship, and came to admire him a great deal. "He was a born leader," he said, as he recalled an incident when they were eleven. Visitors were constantly stopping at the Gore farm to check on or purchase or sell cattle. Often the livestock dealers would bring their children, and Gore and Pope would challenge them to a football game.

"When we were eleven, the two guys we were playing were two or three years older than we were. We were getting beat up pretty bad, scorewise and physical too. They scored several times on us and after about a half hour we both had bloody noses and scratches and even a few tears were flowing. We had possession of the ball close to the hackberry tree, which was one of the goal lines. I told Al that I was getting tired of getting beat up, and not ever scoring. He said, 'So am I, we're going to score this time,' and outlined a plan, which called for Al, who was bigger, to block. He took out one guy. I ran the football and could outrun the other one for a few yards at a time. The last time we huddled, Al told me to go back and throw the ball as far as I could and he would run under it. We did. I took the ball and took off with the big guy right on my heels. Lucky for me, he fell down, so I stopped and threw the ball as far as I could. The defender was caught off guard. Al caught the ball and ran toward the gravel road, which was the other goal line. The boy caught Al before he got to the road. Al was so determined to score that he literally dragged the guy across the road. We went home happy, in spite of the scratches and bloody noses."

"I thought about this," Terry Pope continued, "when I was a senior at Smith County High and Al came home to see me play in the game

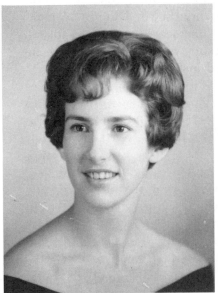 

Donna Armistead Rankin   Donna Armistead Rankin

against our arch-rival, Gordonsville. We were getting whipped pretty good until I saw him standing on the sidelines, and I remembered how he and I played the big boys in the cow pastures."

*   *   *

It was early in the summer of 1962, and Al Gore hadn't been back in Carthage long when he asked to speak to her. "I'd like to take you to a movie, perhaps to Cookeville to the drive-in," he said, "but I can't drive after dark. The driver's license I've got is only good during the day." He stood before her, shifting his weight from one leg to the other, his eyes rolled upward as if he were searching the sky. For a moment, she thought he might be overcome by an attack of nervousness.

Donna Armistead Rankin was about to turn sixteen, and she wondered what her friends at Smith County High would think if they knew she'd dated a fourteen-year-old. She knew his age because he was a friend of her brother, Steve Armistead, but she hadn't considered dating him. She had her own set of friends, was a star player on the Smith County High basketball team, but wondered what a date with a St. Albans student might be like.

Donna thought a moment before answering. He was attractive, came from a good family—but fourteen, and couldn't drive after dark? When she realized she had no license either, the situation became so ludicrous that she thought for a moment she might burst out laughing.

Donna Armistead Rankin

"Okay, I'll go," she said. "I'll get Roy to drive and double with us." Roy was her older brother.

The next night Roy and his date drove them to the Cookeville Drive-In, where she and Al Gore talked all the way through the movie. She can't recall the name of the movie, but they talked about their futures, farming, their friends, Carthage, family and schools for over two hours. She says that she was deeply impressed.

Since her brother was driving them that night, they dropped Al off at the Gore home. He insisted that she come inside and meet his mother. "Come on, come on in with me," he said, and they went inside. Pauline Gore received her graciously and introduced her to a relative who managed the Fairfax Hotel, where the Gores lived in Washington. It was the first of many times that Donna Armistead would visit the Gore family home.

Al took summer courses each year at Castle Heights Military Academy at Lebanon, a small town in Wilson County about twenty miles away. Normally, these were in the fields of political science, government, politics and typing. After he returned from school the next day after his first date with Donna, he came to her grandparents' home, where she lived. Floyd and Edna Armistead operated a country store in Elmwood.

When Al and Donna were alone, Al spoke very carefully, very

deliberately, but directly to the subject. "I wonder if you'd consider not going with anyone but me," he said.

"You mean, like going steady?" she asked.

"Yes, that's what I mean. Going steady. Will you?"

"I don't know, Al, I really don't. You know that our revival is going on at church, and I'm sure someone's going to ask me to go some this week," she told him.

"Please," he begged.

"I'll think about it," she said, "and let you know tonight at church." The young lover left.

That night Al attended services. Afterward he asked her, "Have you even thought about it?"

She replied, "Well, Al, you know. . . ."

From that moment on, throughout her high school years, until they broke up years later, she never dated anyone else. Her high school friends understood. Though Al attended school and lived 650 miles away approximately half of each year, theirs was a pleasant and comfortable relationship.

From the time they began going steady, Donna and her family became closely connected and involved with Al's family. Al, however, became more a part of the daily routine of the Armisteads than the opposite, more like a family member, involved in all Armistead family functions. "He was lost if we were 'out of pocket," Donna said.

The Armistead family was received warmly by the Gore family. "Mr. and Mrs. Gore wanted the best for us. They supported and encouraged us," Donna recalled.

When Donna began dating Al, she joined a social circle that included her brother Steve; Edd Blair, now a Tennessee Highway Patrol sergeant; and Gordon Thompson. Their social life was centered in the New Salem Baptist Church, about a mile east of the Gore farm on Highway 70N.

From the day she became his steady girlfriend and through high school, Donna knew Al Gore better than anyone else, as he shared his thoughts and life with her. He wrote her every day, sometimes two letters a day, and called each Saturday night. At one time she accumulated over five hundred letters, but she has burned all but one.

Donna says that for anyone to understand Al and his family, it's important to remember that he grew up in a busy family. His mother was in New York a great deal of the time in connection with a position she held with the United Nations. She also traveled frequently with her husband, who, as an important U.S. senator, was extremely busy and flew in and out of New York on a regular basis. Nancy was beginning a career in the Peace Corps and traveled throughout the world. Later, after she took a job in Europe, she was seldom in Carthage.

The two people Al Gore Jr. depended on most in Carthage at that period were Donna and Mattie Lucy Payne, but Donna's recollection is that he spent a great deal of time alone on the farm.

Mrs. Gore, however, was careful to ensure that Donna and Al were carefully chaperoned in those years, which amused them both a great deal and resulted, she added laughingly, in "many games to be played." She and Al were lectured periodically by her parents, her grandparents and Pauline Gore, too, but "we had a life that we wanted; we had goals and weren't about to throw them down the drain. We had very nice, normal teenage years. We had responsibility. We were just clean-cut kids," she recalls, complaining that many who've interviewed her for articles about Gore "just don't want to accept that."

She recalls favorably the hospitality that Senator Gore and Pauline showed to her in those years, opening their home to her, her family and friends. She recalls many happy hours in their large cliffside home with its spacious den, eating outstanding food prepared by Mattie Lucy Payne, listening to records and talking to Al. The Gore home became a favorite meeting place for Steve, Edd, Gordon and their dates. In those years she became very close to Mattie Payne and Nancy Gore, both of whom she admired and loved deeply. "Nancy," she said, "was a free spirit, a rare person who treated everyone with the same respect. I loved her a great deal."

Checkers was a favorite game at the Gore home, and Al excelled at it. A family friend, an old judge, came there often. He liked to talk politics and play checkers, Donna recalls.

She was usually a part of the Gore entourage at the time. One evening, while she was visiting there, a farm field caught on fire and there was danger of its spreading. She joined in the firefighting and discovered after it was over that her entire body was covered with soot.

During the months he was in Washington, Al often expressed his desire to "get back home, back to normal." She said he had his bags packed at least two weeks before school was out each spring. She believes he spent far more time in Tennessee in those years than in Washington, taking into account the summers, Thanksgiving and Christmas holidays and special visits.

During those years all her brothers at various times worked on the Gore farm, and worked side by side with Al. The Armistead family did not live on the Gore farm, nor did their group spend much time in Carthage, three miles away. They stayed near home, in the Elmwood community, where the Armistead store was, where the B & B Drive-In was the favorite eating place, where the New Salem Baptist Church was the central social gathering place, and where the Caney Fork River provided much of their recreation.

Donna laughs at the "Doonesbury" characterization of Al Gore as Prince Albert. "Anyone who would say that certainly didn't know the Al Gore I knew," she said. "His father made him work on the farm, showing cattle, working the fields, taking up hay, chopping tobacco. He did it all. He always had one special summer project to complete each year. One year the Senator gave him a small handaxe and told him he had to clear a field that was overgrown with trees and shrubs."

"It nearly killed him, but he finished it that summer," she said. "It was backbreaking work with a tool far too small for the job, but his father wanted him to learn work and the work ethic. The Senator never allowed him to 'sleep in,' and many days he and the farm hands worked from sunup until dark."

"He had little or no money to date on," she recalled.

In her opinion, Al's upbringing was as much like that of a man in the 1930's as possible,' she said. "If it was not absolutely necessary, he didn't get it. If he didn't work it out, it wasn't there for him.

"He didn't have a new car, though of course his parents could have afforded one. When we ran around together, the only car he ever had was a beige, off-white Studebaker stationwagon, his family's car, which he 'flipped' once. He drove the Studebaker until it fell apart."

When he was sixteen, he and Donna were returning to Elmwood from a water-skiing outing at nearby Center Hill Lake. Gore, driving the old Studebaker family stationwagon, stopped and offered a ride to a man and wife who were walking down the highway.

"We'd be much obliged for a ride to Carthage," the pair said as they entered the old Studebaker.

Though it was six miles out of his way, Gore, still not recognized by the couple, told them he'd be happy to take them there. As they approached the Gore farm, very recognizable because of the large cow-shaped sign with huge letters spelling "GORE FARMS," the old lady in the back seat said in her best Tennessee drawl, "Y'all know somethin'? I never could stand that Albert Gore."

Donna looked at the son of the man to whom the lady had referred, but he motioned for her to say nothing. Then, in a tribute to the musical prowess of the elder Gore, her husband remarked, "Yeah, he just fiddled his way right to the Senate." The lady nodded. When Donna turned again to check young Gore's reaction, he burst into uncontrollable laughter that lasted until he had deposited the couple at their destination in Carthage.

Later the Gores bought a Chrysler, but Al never drove it except to the airport to pick up visitors or the Senator. She recalls the Senator's driving speeds, which she said were fast and faster. He always took the wheel when he was picked up at the airport, and she and Al delighted in getting into the back seat, clowning about his driving habits and diving for cover when he'd nearly crash the car—a common occurrence.

Though near-genius and conversant with the theory of quantum physics, he was never good at anything mechanical. Once he and Donna had a flat tire on the way home from a dance at her high school. Al was unable to get the spare out of its compartment, or the wheel off the vehicle, until Donna took charge of the situation and flagged down a carload of her school friends. As Al stood helplessly by, Donna and two of the boys placed the spare on the car, chuckling all the while under their breath about his lack of mechanical ability.

She recalls Al's enthusiasm for sports and his proficiency as a water-skier. "We had a pair of trick skis. Everybody, including my brothers, Gordon, and Edd, would try to outperform the next skier," she said. "We didn't have our own boat to pull us. We'd just sit on the bank until someone friendly enough to give us a tow would come along."

An exceptional basketball player in her own right, she recalls his basketball ability as "terrific." "He could have gotten a basketball scholarship to North Carolina or a bigger school. He was that good. He was good at anything he went after—basketball, football, track, anything that he put his mind to." She recalled that during the time they dated they were both active high school athletes in training, and both refused to drink or smoke.

She is disappointed that many of the articles written about him depict him as being programmed by his father. In her words, "Al is not programmable. His father would have less to do with his decisions than anyone else. He would listen to his father but not always take his advice. Even as a kid he would do that."

"One interviewer," she said, "complained that 'the way you tell it he doesn't have any faults.'"

"Of course he has faults," she said she told him, "but he is just as I've told you, and you now know Al Gore as a young man growing up." The interviewer shook his head and said, "The guy's too good to be true."

"I think he would make a tremendous president," Donna said, with obvious sincerity. "He completely dedicates himself to people he loves, and like most of the people here in Smith County, I plan to support and vote for him. I know he has a wonderful marriage and four beautiful children." She sighs. Regrets? "None," she answers emphatically.

"I'm where I want to be. In Carthage," she says, smiling.

*   *   *

Bonnie McKinney and Jerre McKinney agreed to stop frying hamburgers and dishing out french fries long enough to talk about Al

Steve Armistead

Gordon Thompson

Gore, but "only because it's Al," they said in unison. They run the B & B Drive-In, a small country restaurant about a mile east of the Gore farms on Highway 70N, where you can still get a cheeseburger, french fries and coke for under two dollars.

Bonnie McKinney was carrying one of her diners these items from her menu when she stopped, lifted the plate to eye level, then exclaimed, "Lord, honey, this here was Al's favorite meal. I've cooked hundreds of these for him."

She said she felt she had been a second mother to Al because he practically grew up in her place. "Al and his friends made the B & B their headquarters," she said, "and if one of them came in, it wouldn't be long until Al Gore, Donna, Edd Blair, Goat Thompson, the Pope boy, and maybe Steve and several other Armisteads would join them in a booth. They were great kids growing up out here in the country."

"Al felt at home here," she said. "I could always tell when Senator Gore and Pauline were in Carthage because Al would come here, looking for something to eat."

"Al liked to get away from Washington so he could come home, fish and swim, and be with his friends. They water-skied, drove around in cars and just had fun being young and in the country," she said. "I like him, I know he's a good boy, never been in any trouble anywhere, and will make a wonderful president."

"He liked banana milkshakes too," Jerre McKinney interjected. "That boy was hungry all the time."

Bonnie McKinney   B & B Drive-In

When Sergeant Edd Blair joined the Tennessee Highway Patrol over twelve years ago, he took a lot of ribbing from his old friends about becoming a "Sergeant Joe Friday," or as Donna says, lovingly, a "Barney." But in Smith County, where he knows almost everyone, the 240-pound rock-solid Sergeant Blair is the law, and when he looks at you, you tend to start fumbling through your billfold for your license.

"I wouldn't turn this country over to just anybody," he said, "but I know Al Gore and know you can always trust him to do the right thing. I see him a lot now when he comes back." He smiled proudly. "I'm usually on his security detail, and I like to be around him."

He continued, "I first met him when he was twelve to fourteen years old, and I helped him out cutting some tobacco and hauling some hay. I think I got my driver's license a little bit before he did.

"We just basically ran round together and did the same things that other kids did. He wasn't raised with a silver spoon in his mouth. I've had reporters talk to me and ask if I was embarrassed when I ran around with him because they thought he had a fancy sports car or something. If he had one, I never did see it. He had an old '59 or '60 Studebaker stationwagon. That was his mother and father's car. He did like all the rest of us. We couldn't afford cars. We drove their cars. He never had any more money to spend than we had."

Blair continued, "If we went out on a date, we would pool our

Edd Blair

resources. If we had enough money for a coke we were doing good. What money he had he basically worked on the farm for; he wasn't given none. He worked on the farm and helped other people on occasions haul hay and cut tobacco, whatever. That was about the only way he had of getting any spending money."

"Now, he did get a good education at some good prep schools and I'm glad he did," he said. "But the fact that he graduated from Harvard didn't change him. He's just one of the people, who was lucky enough to get ahead, but he's kept his roots here.

"The first car he ever owned was a Firebird that he bought new after he got out of school. This was just a short time before he went into the service. I don't remember where he got it, but it was red and had a white vinyl top."

"Donna Armistead, who's now a Rankin, is the only girl I ever knew he went with," Edd Blair said.

"Now, as to a sense of humor, he's basically pretty serious all the time about everything. It was just his nature ever since I can remember him. He's been a lot more serious than some of the rest of us around. He took a lot of things serious where we didn't. He had an accident in his parents' Studebaker once. We would all go too fast to see which one could get to Carthage or the B & B the quickest."

Blair said, "He's on a health kick now, don't drink coffee or anything with caffeine in it, but growing up we all drank cokes, ate hamburgers — his favorite food then.

"Far back as I can remember, he went to New Salem Missionary Baptist Church. . . . I don't worry too much about that marijuana thing. Never did it around me. I was with him pretty often when he moved back to Nashville working at *The Tennessean,* and he couldn't have done it much because I was with him a lot of the time. I think he did it a little in Vietnam, like most of the boys did. That's over and probably never was much to it.

"Well, our group was Al, Donna, her brother Steve, me, Goat Thompson, and Terry Pope. We were just country kids who threw rocks, ran races, water-skied, played and worked hard.

"That's what Al Gore did growing up, and that's Al Gore. I think he'll make a good president. He's sincere about everything he does. He wants to help people, the needy especially, and I think he will help strengthen Social Security. He has spent a lot of time learning about nuclear arms and probably knows more about it than anybody running. I don't know of anything that would disqualify him for president. He works hard at anything he goes after. When we were growing up, we might give it our best for a little while and then slack off. Not Al. It didn't matter whether we were playing ball or just 'I can beat you from here to there.' He gave it 110 percent and the rest of us didn't.

"He married a fine woman, and they both do what they think is right.

"I think he's the best America can produce."

*   *   *

In addition to the excellent preparatory school education young Al Gore received at St. Albans, Pauline Gore saw to it that he was exposed to the cultural and governmental benefits of Washington, D.C., including the Library of Congress, museums and cultural halls, the Smithsonian Institute, the White House, the Archives, plays, the zoo, and government agencies.

St. Albans School for Boys is one of the ten best preparatory schools in America, and there the foundation for Gore's excellent scholastic record was laid. He began in the elementary section in the fourth grade and completed Lower Form, which is through the eighth grade. In Lower School, Gore concentrated on English, mathematics, history, science, religion, foreign language, art and music.

In the Upper School, or the high school department, Gore's graduation requirements consisted of four years of English, three and a half years

New Salem Missionary Baptist Church

of a foreign language (or three of one and two of another), two semesters of religion, one semester of computer science, two years of history, and at least three years of mathematics through precalculus. He was allowed some electives, and in these he concentrated on painting and creative writing.

Although competing with some of the most intelligent and gifted students in the nation, Gore was able to maintain a scholastic record which netted him a National Merit Award Scholarship to Harvard.

He was class treasurer in his freshman and sophomore years. Active in the Government Club the two years prior to graduation, he was elected Liberal Party Leader his senior year. He was a member of the Glee Club for three years prior to graduation and served on the Student Council his junior year.

During his junior and senior years he was a prefect, a student leader, and a member of the Athletic Association. His special interests at St. Albans included art, politics, agriculture and Tennessee.

Gore lettered in football his sophomore, junior and senior years. He was captain of the football team his senior year. He also lettered in basketball the last four years and in track the last three.

During the fall of 1964 young Gore captained his football team, the same time his father was engaged in a bitter re-election campaign for

Al and his calf

Nancy, Pauline and Al

his Senate seat in Tennessee against Memphis Republican Dan Kuykendall. When Senator Gore stood victorious before his supporters on election night in early November, he said, "My son is a senior in high school and captain of the football team, and I haven't seen him play a game all season. I'm going to be there for homecoming Friday night." And he was.

As captain of the football team, Al Gore was unselfish, a team member who wanted to win for the school above all. He gave complete dedication to the team and its success. He was an unselfish member of the basketball team. His coach said he stayed after other team members had left the gymnasium, perfecting his jump shot, trying to get better. [5]

On the day of any important athletic contest, he always wanted the same breakfast—steak, biscuits and white gravy. [6]

Gore had two nicknames at St. Albans. Though he preferred to be called Al, some of his schoolmates stuck him with "Gorf."

Al boarded at St. Albans during his last years there. His roommate at St. Albans told Knight-Ridder reporter Nolan Walters that in regard to Gore's presidential bid, "Those of us who knew Al knew that this was inevitable. The script was written twenty-one years ago." [7]

Under his senior class picture in the 1965 yearbook, a prophetic member of the yearbook staff penned this message: "Al is frighteningly good at many things. Varsity football Captain, basketball and track standout, Liberal Party Leader in Government Class, scholar, artist

St. Albans School for Boys

extraordinary, Al has stood out in many fields of endeavor. Popular and respected he would seem the epitome of the All-American Young Man. It probably won't be long before Al reaches the top. When he does, all of his classmates will remark to themselves, 'I knew that guy was going somewhere in life.'"[8]

Canon Charles Martin was headmaster during the nine years Al Gore was enrolled at St. Albans and observed the youth grow into manhood from 1954 to 1965. He thinks highly of Gore's potential, which he and the school saw early as Al filled leadership roles in both athletics and academics. Gore was "the Tennessee boy" to Headmaster Martin, who as Canon Martin would later perform Tipper and Al's wedding ceremony at the Washington Cathedral.

Canon Martin said, "Al Gore was born to lead and nurtured to lead by his family. His mother and father, each in quite different ways, are remarkable people. And so is his wife, Tipper.

"His sister, I knew only slightly but I know how much she meant to Al and to the rest of the family. Her death was a great tragedy to all of them.

"Al was at St. Albans for nine years and did a fine job. With his left hand he did his studies and was at the top of the heap; with his right he was captain in football and good in basketball, track, and baseball.

Canon Charles Martin

More, he was a vestryman, a prefect. The boys recognized him as a leader and, interestingly enough, predicted he would be President of the United States!"

*   *   *

As the youth finished his high school career at St. Albans in 1965, he attended the school's party for its graduates. With money he had received in gifts for graduation and some he'd saved, he bought the brightest red Pontiac Firebird he could find.

He was about to meet someone at the party who would affect his life dramatically.

Al Gore—track, St. Albans
(1964)

Al Gore—No. 50, St. Albans
basketball (1964)

St. Albans basketball team
(1964)

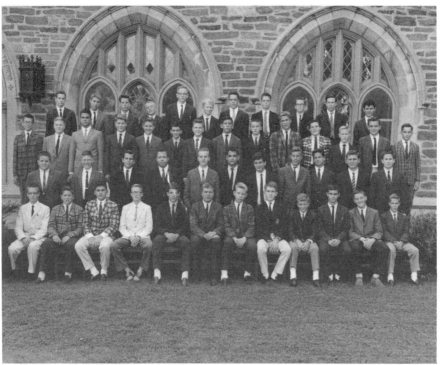

St. Albans class (1964)

Al Gore Jr. (St. Albans track)

Mattie Lucy Payne (1988)

Jerry Thompson

Chapter Four

O God, who hast revealed Thyself in the glory of the heavens and in the burning bush, in the still small voice, and in the dread power of the hydrogen bomb; make us aware of Thy presence as Thou comest in judgment through the events of our time.

Grant us to stand in awe to sin not. Enable us to use the fearful powers Thou hast permitted us to know that we may work not toward man's destruction but toward his fulfillment.

Lift us above the suspicions and fears of our day that we may bring righteous and just peace among all men. And this we ask, anxious, yet quiet in Thee; perplexed, yet certain in Thee; weak, yet strong in Thee, through Him who is the savior of us all, Jesus Christ our Lord. Amen.[1]

Charles Martin
Headmaster
St. Albans, 1949-1977

During their television interview on David Frost's program, they described their meeting in May 1965 as "very fleeting"; however, the introductions that occurred between Tipper and Al Gore at the St. Albans School for Boys graduation party changed their lives forever. Both said they were there with other dates. She was finishing her junior year at St. Agnes Episcopal School for Girls in Alexandria, Virginia. [2]

Al Gore, 17, remembered that there "was something special about her, and how pretty she was."

The next day, Al called her. "I'm Al Gore," he said. "Do you remember me from last night?"

"Sure," Tipper said, "I sure do." And why not? Al Gore had stood out at the party. Tall, handsome, with black hair and a voice that commanded attention, with a slight Southern accent highlighted with

Al and Tipper at the farm

Tipper and Al (1965)

cultured St. Albans finishing touches. Since their meeting, she'd also learned that he'd captained his football team and starred on the basketball team the past four years.

And though she didn't mention it, last night had not been the first time Tipper had heard of Al Gore. The son of a famous U.S. senator who was in the news much of the time with his opposition to the Vietnam War, young Gore had been the topic of numerous telephone conversations among the young debutantes who attended private and parochial schools in and around the District of Columbia.

In their own words, they were "pretty much taken with one another" from the time of their first date. They went to a neighborhood movie, and began a courtship that lasted for the next five years.

Her name was Mary Elizabeth Aitcheson, but she'd had the nickname "Tipper" since she was a small child. She was sixteen, liked rock and roll music and was "pretty good" on a set of drums. For most of the time since her parents divorced when she was three, Tipper had lived with her mother, Margaret Ann Carlson Aitcheson, in a Tudor style home they shared with her grandparents at 1201 26th Street South in Arlington.[3]

Though her husband prefers to call her Mary Elizabeth, Tipper believes she is "stuck" with the nickname, the origin of which she explained to David Frost:

"There was an old Spanish ballad that my mother liked, and she sang it to me when I was little. I was sick, and this song was the only thing

Arlington home where Tipper
grew up; now the Al Gore
home

Tipper Gore (1988)

I responded to. It's called 'Tippy Tippy Tin.' So she nicknamed me after
it. It's worn well. . . . I've had it so long and it looks like it will stick,
so I must like it."[4]

After her parents divorced, not seeing her father often was painful
for the young girl. Tipper's father, John Kenneth Aitcheson Jr., however,
did maintain contact with her through the years and spoke lovingly of
her in a report on a Nashville TV station after Gore's candidacy
announcement. He is the son of John Kenneth and Virginia Dare Clarke
Aitcheson, an old, established Alexandria, Virginia, family that
maintained a residence for years on West Oak Street.

Since it was only blocks from her high school, Tipper was fond of
the home her grandparents, the Carlsons, owned in Arlington. In 1977,
she and her husband purchased and moved into this home, which she
described for a Nashville newspaper in 1987:

"It was built in 1938 by my grandparents. It's a brick, English Tudor-
style house. I spent a lot of time growing up there. . . . Karenna, my
oldest daughter, has my old bedroom. We. . . put an addition all across
the back. It's a very modern addition with cathedral ceilings and lots
of glass. We love it. We're five minutes from National Airport and ten
minutes from Capitol Hill. I think there's six bedrooms now."[5]

John Tyson   Al Gore

*   *   *

September 1965 was a difficult time for a youth of seventeen in America. Twenty-two months earlier the nation had undergone its first presidential assassination since 1901 (President William McKinley's murder); racial tension and suspicion were at an all-time high; draft quotas were high; military desertion rates had skyrocketed; and America had a president with a reputation for double-dealing and questionable financial connections. The same president had assured the nation months earlier, during his re-election campaign of 1964, that he had no plans to widen the scope of America's involvement in the war, and saw no reason to send additional U.S. troops into the conflict.

Immediately after his election, President Johnson began shipping American troops into Vietnam in one of the most massive military build-ups in American history. The toll of those injured and killed was staggering, especially in the face of advice of military experts who had said for decades that a land war in Asia could not be won.

This was the backdrop for Al Gore's enrollment at Harvard University in September 1965. Armed with financial aid he'd won in the National Merit Award Scholarship, Al Gore wasted little time in announcing his candidacy for freshman class president after he arrived at Cambridge. Certainly there was no one in the class who could match his experience in planning and carrying out successful political campaigns.

John Tyson stems from a prominent black family in Montclair, New Jersey. Now a successful investment banker and still a close friend and supporter of Al Gore's, he met the young Southern white boy a few days after he arrived on campus. After they had established their friendship, Gore asked to room with him the next year and did. Tyson spoke recently with a reporter on the MacNeil/Lehrer TV News Report about Al Gore:

"I met Al Gore our freshman year when he came and knocked on the door; I opened the door and there he stood. He said, 'Hi, I'm Al Gore. I'm running for freshman council.' That's how I met Al Gore." [6]

"Tyson was so impressed," commented the reporter, "he voted for Gore even though his roommate was running for the same office. The following year Tyson was sharing a room with the young Southerner." [7]

"Al was my kind of guy," Tyson continued. "I remember playing football and Al would take his motorcycle out to the airport and pick up my sister and put her on the back of his motorcycle and drive—ride through—remember this is in Boston in the 1960's." [8]

Tyson told Gail Sheehy of *Vanity Fair* recently that "the most important thing I learned from Al was not to be prejudiced myself." [9]

After a spirited contest, Gore won election as freshman class president and served with distinction in the post.

Surprisingly, one of the things that endeared him to many students on the staid Harvard campus was the used motorcycle he purchased and brought back to school after the first Christmas break. The helmeted Gore became a familiar sight, often intentionally "revving" the engine as he passed certain buildings, but generally he enjoyed riding in the countryside. There he was free to let the cycle go, and he could see the land, could feel the wind whipping around him as he went up and down the coastline.

During Gore's freshman year at Harvard, he and Tipper corresponded regularly. Since she would graduate from St. Agnes the next spring, Al asked her to find a college in or near Boston, so that they could be together.

To conduct her investigation, she recruited her grandmother to drive to Boston during the spring break of 1966. Commenting on their stay at the Copley Plaza, Tipper laughed and said, "It was so I could visit Al and be chaperoned. Sounds like ancient history, doesn't it." [10]

She selected Garland College, a junior college in Boston, and enrolled the following September. Graduating *cum laude* two years later, she transferred to Boston University, where she majored in child psychology and received her bachelor's degree in 1970.

After Tipper arrived in Boston, she became acquainted with several of Gore's Harvard professors. She and Gore spent considerable time

Al Gore   John Tyson

with Dr. Martin Peretz, who even then recognized potential in the youth. Later, when Gore announced his candidacy, Dr. Peretz, then editor-in-chief of *New Republic,* endorsed Gore and published a number of articles favorable to his candidacy.

Gore also came under the tutelage of Dr. Richard Neustadt, a renowned expert on presidential power, who supervised Gore's writing of his senior thesis. Titled "The Impact of Television on the Conduct of the Presidency, 1947-1969," the 103-page treatise dealt extensively with presidential debates and their effect on elections to that time.

*   *   *

In the summers of Gore's tenure at Harvard, he increasingly found less time to spend in Carthage. He worked one summer in Brussels. During another he took a full load of college work in Mexico City, where he became so proficient in Spanish that he was able to translate later for his father in a visit to a Spanish-American neighborhood. He even took courses in Tennessee history in Memphis, and he worked one summer as a copyboy for the *New York Times.*

In the meantime, he and Donna Armistead drifted apart, and she married soon after their romance terminated.

Dr. Charles Crawford is chairman of the Oral Research (History) Department at Memphis State University, where, during the summer break of 1968, he taught Al Gore Jr. in a Tennessee history course.

"Young Gore was an exceptional student," he recalled, "very motivated, vitally interested in the history of our state."

"I came to know him very well that summer," Dr. Crawford recalled, "and when the call came for volunteers to assist in his New Hampshire effort, I signed up and worked for him there. He is an excellent young man, well qualified for high leadership."

Al Gore was in Tennessee in March 1966 for several reasons. Though in no immediate danger of being drafted, since he was a student, he had to comply with the law by registering on his eighteenth birthday with his hometown Selective Service Board. Dutifully, he executed the forms, swore they were true and then was issued a draft card. A number of his friends in Carthage, including Steve Armistead, had told him that he could forget about a political career in Tennessee if he avoided military service.

Gore was in Carthage that day for another reason. Under the law in Tennessee at the time, persons under twenty-one years of age could not contract, make deeds, sue or be sued, or engage in certain occupations, unless an authorized chancery court "removed this disability of minority." On March 31, 1966, Gore petitioned Chancellor Scott Camp of the Smith County Chancery Court to remove his "disability of minority" pursuant to Section 23-1201, Et. Sec., Tennessee Code Annotated, to allow him to sign documents in companies in which he held stock, and to purchase shares of stock in GoRay Realty Company. His parents, B. Clark Meadows, Reba G. Harper and Katherine S. Beasley joined in the request. The next day, Chancellor Scott Camp granted Gore the relief sought.

Later that day, toward dusk, Al Gore drove to the top of a hill that would allow him to see the long stretch of dark river bottom land that ran along the river and Highway 25 a few miles from Carthage. He gazed for several minutes from his vantage point, then said, "I bought this land today, but I owe more money on it than I ever thought possible. Here I am, eighteen and owe all this money. How am I ever going to pay it off?"

Though he was concerned, Gore had made a wise purchase. Later a company in which he was to become a principal, Tanglewood Home Builders Inc., would develop the property into building lots that were sold to individuals or to the family corporation.

* * *

Although Tipper made an immediate and permanent impression on the entire Gore family, she did not visit the Gore farm until 1967. Strikingly attractive, slim, blonde, and socially correct in every way,

Tipper captivated the Gores and their Tennessee neighbors and associates. Pauline Gore told her recollections of Tipper and her visit in a cookbook she published in 1984:

"Mary Elizabeth ('Tipper') Aitcheson of Arlington, Va., is a descendant of a West Tennessee family, her grandmother having been born in Weakley County, where I had my nativity, too. We first heard of her after Al had met her at some school occasion. Right off, I could tell, he developed a growing, if not an abiding, interest in her. She came to our house in Smith County, Tennessee, for a weekend visit in 1967. Very young, beautiful and cheerful, she brightened life in the entire household.

"Al had arranged a special gift for her coming—a baby skunk with a long white stripe down its back from nose to tip of tail, otherwise very black. Al had found it on the farm the weekend before, and meanwhile, had taken it to our local veterinarian for 'defumigating.' Then, he and our daughter Nancy had bathed and babied it for a week until, despite my husband's misgivings, it was as cute as one could ever see.

"Tipper was excited and expressed great delight with it. She stroked and cuddled it with tender loving care. She named it 'Mandy.'

"I gave Tipper a box for its bed, and she bedded the box with shredded tissue paper.

"Mattie had prepared fried chicken for dinner, and she told us it was ready. So, Tipper placed 'Mandy' in its box; Al tied the lid on with a ribbon and placed it on the back porch.

"Mattie's fried chicken and vegetable dinner was, as usual, delicious. All things went well until it was discovered that while we were eating dinner 'Mandy' had gnawed out of the box and escaped into the darkness.

"Tipper was crushed, saying 'that was my only pet.' This stirred Al to activity. 'I think I can find it,' he said, grabbing a flashlight and making for the door.

"'Wait,' Tipper said, 'I want to go too.' So off they wandered into the darkness, scouring every niche, bush and corner with the flashlight.

"After about an hour they returned triumphant, Tipper aglow with pride and cuddling her possession. Al, too, seemed pretty well satisfied with himself.

"Tipper sat in a lounge chair in the living room and placed her pet on the arm of the chair.

"Suddenly Albert shouted, 'That's not the same skunk; its stripe is short. Take it outside quick.'

"Simultaneously, Tipper jumped up; Al grabbed the little polecat which exploded its native bomb.

"Everyone, including Mattie, rushed out of the house, leaving all doors open through one of which the little polecat made the second escape of the evening."[11]

*   *   *

Gore's tenure (1965-69) at Harvard became a time of turmoil. Students opposed to U.S. involvement in Vietnam occupied the administration building, staged a strike, and burned their draft cards. Young Gore, who at one time had considered West Point and a military career, was never in the mainstream of protest on the campus, although he opposed the Vietnam War. Gore realized that these activities could pose a problem if he ever decided to enter politics, an option he often talked about in those days.

The elder Gore was then a member of the Senate Foreign Relations Committee and daily expressed his displeasure at U.S. involvement and was particularly incensed when he heard news reports which conflicted with confidential and accurate information he was receiving in his official capacity. Senator Gore Sr. believed the American people were being lied to and misled by the government about what was occurring in Vietnam.

Again the voice of John Tyson, Gore's Harvard roommate, on the MacNeil/Lehrer Report: "At that time his father was our real champion on the foreign relations committee in the Senate. Al was sought after, so to speak, by a lot of the radicals to join up with them and to give them information in terms of what his insights were, his political thoughts on the matter. But when things got too far, his sense—he's got good sense—when he sensed that things were getting out of proportion—out of balance—he shied away from those people."[12]

In the spring of 1969, Gore was graduated from Harvard with a BA degree *cum laude* in government. He left Tipper in Boston to complete another school year at Boston University. The war in Vietnam continued to rage, and as the young man looked toward returning to Carthage, where his draft board was located, he realized there was nothing to prevent him from being inducted into military service.

Tipper Gore (1988; photo by Owen Cartwright, courtesy *Nashville Banner*)

Al Gore Jr. shows prize Angus, Iowa, 1987 (photo by Bruce Dobie, courtesy *Nashville Banner*)

Tipper and Al Gore Jr. and Gore children (1987; photo by Bill Thorup, courtesy *Nashville Banner*)

Chapter Five

"The first duty of a soldier or good citizen is to attend to the safety or interest of his country."
President Andrew Jackson, letter to Henry Dearborn, January 8,1807.

With his education completed at Harvard, Gore realized that he had no more than two months before his draft board at Carthage issued orders to induct him into military service. He could understand the pressure his draft board was probably under from the Selective Service System. Replacements were needed in Vietnam because the war was going badly, casualties were high, and there were large numbers of draft evaders and military deserters.

And Carthage was a small town, where Gore knew all the members of the draft board. If he did anything out of the ordinary to avoid military service, the word would spread through the county, then across the state, probably mortally wounding his father's chances for re-election in 1970. Newspapers and political experts were already predicting Albert Sr.'s political demise because he had opposed the Vietnam War so vehemently.

Gore was trapped in a catch-22 situation. If he could succeed in having his name removed from the pool of prospective inductees, by claiming conscientious objector status, or by teaching school, or by coming up with an injury that would merit 4-F classification, someone would have to take his place, and perhaps a friend would be forced to replace him.

He has said repeatedly that it "was one of the most difficult decisions that I've ever had to make."

"I wasn't totally sure at the time that it was the right decision, but I feel now that it was the right decision," Gore said recently. "I'm glad that I made that decision, and I would do it over again.."[1]

Al and Albert Gore (Photo by
Jack Gunter, courtesy *Nashville
Banner*)

Al Gore, U.S. Army

Gore turned to his parents for advice. They say that they tried in every
way to keep that decision free of any influence the decision would have
on his father's race, and they deny that this aspect was ever mentioned
to their son.

John Tyson's words on the MacNeil/Lehrer Report provide insights
into Gore's thinking at the time: "Al decided that he was going to enlist
and he was helping the anti-war movement more or less by going and
enlisting."[2]

"How would that help?" the interviewer asked.

"Well, in a sense I believe it would have helped his dad. He felt by
helping his dad and campaigning with his dad that that was the greatest
thing he as an individual could do to stop the war." [3]

Gore says his decision to enlist was primarily an ethical not a political
choice. "Everybody knew there was a kind of [draft] quota, and if I didn't
go, then one of my friends would have to go in my place."[4]

He describes his struggle over enlisting as an almost bloodlessly
rational debate between his revulsion against the war and his sense of
duty. That description fits what friends say about Gore's personality;
he has always been a little "stiff collar," as Edd Blair puts it. At both
St. Albans and Harvard, he was more deeply involved in athletics and
academic matters than in political activities.

According to Nolan Walters, Gore said the physical danger was not a consideration. "Maybe I didn't have enough intellectual courage to admit that that was part of the consideration, but it never really did enter consciously into the deliberation," he said.[5]

Like his father, Gore believed the war in Vietnam was illegal and doomed, but he was never involved in the radical movement. He helped write the speech his father gave against the war at the 1968 presidential campaign of peace candidate Eugene McCarthy, and he has acknowledged occasionally smoking marijuana in college and in the Army. But he tended to be on the fringes of protests.

"It is my recollection that Albert didn't want to kill anybody, and it probably bothered him quite a bit to make any contribution to the war effort," said the actor Tommy Lee Jones, one of Gore's college friends.

Many of Al's friends considered similar reservations justification enough to avoid the draft by getting a deferment to teach or to attend divinity school after college.

But Gore's situation was complicated by his father's re-election bid, which had been wounded seriously by the outspoken anti-war views, which his opponent was already telling voters throughout the Volunteer State about.

Pauline and Albert Gore denied on the MacNeil/Lehrer report that any pressure was put on Al to join the Army.

As graduation time approached, Gore turned for advice to his Harvard mentors, including Richard Neustadt, a nationally known authority on presidential power, and Martin Peretz, now editor-in-chief of the *New Republic*, both of whom were concerned that he might do something to damage his future in politics.

After a visit in mid-July to Peretz and Neustadt on Cape Cod, Gore decided to enlist, and a few days later flew from Boston to Newark, a city Gore considered neutral and anonymous.

Gore went to the Army's Newark recruiting station, where he received a battery of tests. Based on his performance, he was assigned duty as an Army journalist.

After basic training in New Jersey, Gore was assigned to Fort Rucker, Alabama, where he would work on the base newspaper.

* * *

As Mary Elizabeth Aitcheson and Albert Arnold Gore Jr. prepared for their wedding at the high altar of the Washington Cathedral in Washington on May 19, 1970, grim news from Vietnam cast a dark shadow on the festive and happy occasion. In the week preceding the wedding, 217 American servicemen were killed in the fighting.

But the families put the war aside for a time and enjoyed the usual

Washington Cathedral, Site of Wedding

teas and parties, the guests and the gifts and the greetings. Tipper was ecstatic. She told a *Nashville Scene* reporter in 1987, "I was just on Cloud Nine. I was getting married, getting ready to go off on our honeymoon, and I don't even remember who was there." [6]

May 19th was sunny and warm throughout the day. Clouds threatened rain late in the afternoon, but after they dispersed, the evening was cool and pleasant.

A number of out-of-town guests and some local political celebrities were expected, and the guests actually began arriving about an hour before the announced 7:00 PM ceremony at the Washington Cathedral, a stone's throw from St. Albans School. The Washington Cathedral was an historic landmark, the scene of numerous weddings, funerals and christenings of famous personages in its decades in northwest Washington, where it stood atop one of the tallest knolls in the city.

Surprisingly, the *Washington Post* left it to the *Alexandria Gazette* to report the details of the wedding:[7]

The church was decorated with beautiful spring flowers. Gore's former headmaster at St. Albans, Canon Charles Martin, performed the formal ceremony, which was conducted at the high altar, the most sacred place in the beautiful building.

The organist, Warren Steele, played both traditional and contemporary musical selections, including at least one selection the Beatles had made famous.

John Kenneth Aitcheson Jr. gave his daughter, Mary Elizabeth, in

Mr. and Mrs. Al Gore Jr. (Photo by Bob Ray, courtesy *Nashvile Banner*)

marriage. She wore an empire gown with long, tapered sleeves and chapel train made of white Alencon lace and peau de soie embroidered in seed pearls, and carried a bouquet of white carnations, babies breath and orchids. A coronet of peau de soie and seed pearls held her veil of illusion and lace.

The groom, Albert Arnold Gore Jr., wore his Army dress uniform.

Tipper's cousin, Page Pettit of McLean, Virginia, served as maid of honor. Gore's sister, Nancy Gore Hunger of Greenville, Mississippi, served as matron of honor.

Bridesmaids were Denise Gibbs of Arlington; Barbara Flannigan of New York City; Tracy Hover of Houston, Texas; and Lee Di Perri of Wiscasset, Maine. The junior bridesmaid was Gail Pettit of McLean, Virginia, Tipper's cousin.

James Gordon Landau of New York City served the groom as best man. Ushers were Mark Gore and Jaime Gore of Washington, Al Gore's cousins; Tommy Lee Jones of Midland, Texas; Bob Somerby of Winchester, Massachusetts; Mike Kapetan of Wayne, Michigan; and Steve Armistead of Hermitage, Tennessee.

The reception which followed the wedding was held at the Belle Haven Country Club.

* * *

After the honeymoon Private Gore and his new bride reported to

Spec. 4 Al Gore Jr. recognized by Maj. Gen. Delk M. Oden, comanding general of Ft. Rucker, Alabama, as Post Soldier of May 1970.

their new duty station at Fort Rucker, Alabama, where Gore would be assigned to the post information office.

When Gore and Tipper arrived at Fort Rucker, the Vietnam War was raging, and the huge Army base deep in the wiregrass section of southern Alabama was alive with activity. It was a principal training post for helicopter pilots and crew personnel; hundreds of Army aviators had to be processed each month to feed the growing need in the combat zones of Vietnam.

And life in the area was Spartan. There were no good restaurants, not even one of the fast food variety, very few family-oriented recreational facilities, and little or no housing to speak of.

As Al and Tipper began to check out places they felt they could afford on his private's pay, she was horrified that American servicemen and their families had to live in places like those that were shown them. At the first trailer park Tipper, trying her best to be a "good soldier" herself, walked confidently into a trailer, went directly to the refrigerator and opened the door.

Tipper fell back, shocked, almost faint. The inside of the refrigerator was, in her words, "so infested with cockroaches you would not believe it. We opened the refrigerator door and it was black until they scattered, then it was white on the inside. I started crying at that point."[8]

They left and went directly to Horsley's Trailer Park, a twelve-acre complex that had been recommended for its cleanliness and appearance.

Ewell and Voncille Horsley have been renting trailers to Army enlisted personnel on a short-term basis since the 1950's. Today they're still in business at Daleville, Alabama, two miles from Fort Rucker Army Base, and recall Al and Tipper as "excellent tenants, and Al as a young man who liked to talk about politics."[9]

At Horsley's they found a trailer on Lot 10 that an Army sergeant owned and was renting. Since it was clean, had no roaches or rodents, they took it immediately. The young Albert Gore family, now with two members and recently married in the nation's most prestigious church, had established their first home in Trailer No. 10, "Expando model," in a huge field at Horsley's Trailer Park in the wiregrass section of southern Alabama.

In the months that came at Fort Rucker, Gore worked hard as a reporter on the base newspaper, painting, taking short trips in the area, and playing basketball with a group of neighbors in the trailer park.

Gore found it relatively easy during his military service to perform in an outstanding manner. With his excellent intellect and in good physical condition, he was able to do anything the military asked of him. The truth of the matter was that Gore was an excellent soldier, an enlisted man who understood and practiced military tradition and courtesy, generally making an excellent military appearance.

In May 1970, Gore was selected as Post Soldier of the Month, based on his knowledge of military subjects, outstanding military bearing, leadership qualities, and courtesy. The commandant of the Army Aviation School, Maj. Gen. Delk M. Oden, commanding general at Ft. Rucker, recognized his achievement in a post ceremony in which he awarded Spec. 4 Gore a $50 U.S. Savings Bond and a letter of commendation.

In early March 1988 Gore returned to Fort Rucker while campaigning in Alabama, and made a nostalgic visit back to see Ewell and Voncille Horsley and the trailer park they still operate. As he looked at the concrete slab that formerly supported Trailer No. 10, Gore told the crowd that had come out to see him that "we were very happy here." "We got to travel," he said, laughingly. "We went to Ozark, Dothan and Enterprise [towns in the area] and even saw the Boll Weevil Monument." The crowd understood and applauded.[10]

"We had a real nice trailer. We had a ten-foot expando in the living room—well, ten feet is exaggerating it a little bit. Maybe it was more like six feet. Was it six feet, Mr. Horsley?"

The trailer park owner nodded in agreement, obviously delighted with the return of his most famous tenant.[11]

As Gore stood under trees which covered the concrete slab that had once supported his home, he reminisced with the crowd. "We have some

Pauline Gore

old snapshots of us standing out here in the back yard," he said, pointing east, "and we had a basketball team that used to play right over there."[12]

"This is a happy visit for me. I think it would be good to land Air Force One right here sometime. If I'm elected, the people of Daleville and the wiregrass section will have a friend in the White House," he said. "I want to put the White House back on the side of the people who live in Horsley's Trailer Park. I want to fashion policies that will be what's best for the PFC at Fort Rucker."[13]

Gore painted a great deal while living in the trailer. He told one interviewer, "Painting is my great emotional catharsis. That's how I filled my time down at Fort Rucker."[14]

*   *   *

While Tipper and Al were in their "Expando" trailer home at Fort Rucker, the elder Senator Gore was in the midst of the toughest re-election try of his political career, trying to fend off the charging Bill Brock and his Republican Party, who wanted Gore's Senate seat. Senator Gore established a campaign headquarters at the Hermitage Hotel in Nashville, just across from the Andrew Jackson Hotel, where he had met Pauline years earlier.

Al came to Tennessee on weekends whenever he could get away and spent most of his pre-Vietnam leave campaigning with other members of the Gore family.

A 1970 campaign event. Left to right: Mayor Richard Fulton, Al, Tipper, Albert Sr., Nancy, Jim Sasser, and Frank Hunger.

Nancy Gore Hunger, her father's campaign manager, recruited her husband, Frank Hunger, virtually to abandon his law practice in Greenville, Mississippi, and campaign in west Tennessee. She recalled her father's strategy in past campaigns: "Once during a campaign when I was about fifteen,... I said to my father, I'm so tired. He told me to banish that word from my vocabulary, tired."[15] "We have a pecking order this family uses in the campaign," she said. "When my father has to cancel an appearance, mother cancels hers to fill it. I cancel mine to fill hers. Tipper cancels hers to fill mine."[16]

Pauline, Nancy and Tipper spoke for the elder Gore wherever they could find an audience that would listen. They appeared at teas, coffees, luncheons, social gatherings, neighborhood parties, Democratic Party rallies, anywhere they could be used. At any given time during the campaign there were four different Gores speaking throughout the state.

Pauline Gore told the *Nashville Tennessean* that her husband's 1970 campaign was the most strenuous of her recollection in their three decades of political life, that they actually began the campaign two years earlier when the results of the 1968 election came in. "We could see then that any Democrat would have a hard time in Tennessee.... Had we not worked so hard, we might have preferred not to make the hard fight. But Albert had worked so long for certain programs and he wanted to see them carried through."[17]

Tipper said, "Al warned me...what it would be like during the campaign. I've had some adjustments to make, naturally. Anyone would have to adjust to the pace this family keeps. College was easy compared to this."[18]

The senior Gore characterized his last campaign as "bitter," but even today he will not personally attack Bill Brock, his opponent. Brock's charges that Senator Gore had lost touch with his state and its voters, had become too liberal in opposing the Vietnam War, touched a responsive chord among the voters of Tennessee.

When it was all over, those voters turned him out of office by over 46,000 votes. In his concession speech on election night, he stood with eyes blazing and said, "Someday, and someday soon. . .I know that the truth. . .shall rise again. . .in Tennessee!"

Many believed that the elder Gore was referring to young Al Gore, who would follow in his footsteps one day, but Al Gore doesn't believe that was his father's intention. He told TV interviewer David Frost that his father's prediction had to do with "humor." Gore said, "It was clear in 1970 that my father was defeated. And yet it was inspirational in that truth shall rise again. I don't think he meant someone in the family would rise again with the truth. After that, people in Tennessee changed their feeling about him dramatically."[19]

John Seigenthaler says, "I think there was great disillusionment because Al looked upon his father as a great, dedicated, caring, sensitive, patriotic public servant, whose record had resulted in making the world safer, and his name was on the interstates that ran across the country, and he had provided support for domestic programs that had made this valley, the Tennessee Valley, a garden spot. And Al Gore felt that his father, on the basis of all that and on the basis of his intelligence and his service, simply deserved to be elected."

*   *   *

When Specialist 5 Albert Gore Jr., 22, finished his pre-Vietnam leave with his family in Tennessee in November 1970, his military orders called for him to report to the 20th Engineer Brigade at the Long Binh military base near Saigon.

During the long flight to South Vietnam, he wondered whether his decision to enlist had been the right one. After all, a number of his Harvard schoolmates had avoided military service, some even burning their draft cards in protest. Many college students of the day had even fled to Canada. Like many Americans, he felt the war was wrong, that U.S. policy there was flawed and misguided. But he could not bring himself to turn his back on his country; his state, Tennessee, the Volunteer State; and his family. When this is all over, he told himself,

Spec. 5 Gore in Vietnam   Tipper Gore

I can walk down the streets of Carthage, or Washington, look anyone I meet in the eye and say to myself that I served my country when I was called, that no one had to serve in my stead.

After he landed at the huge airfield near Saigon, he reported to his unit, which was headquartered nearby. Like every GI stationed in a combat zone, he was issued standard military gear, including an M-16 5.56mm automatic rifle and ammunition.

Once there and into his duties as a combat journalist, Gore soon learned that the war was much meaner and more brutal on both sides than he'd ever imagined, and the issues much more complex and ambiguous than the debate back in the States indicated.

Gore was deeply affected by his Vietnam experiences. He could not accept the atrocities that accompanied almost any tour of duty in Vietnam. As an Army reporter, Gore took his turn regularly on the perimeter in small firebases out in the "boonies" where standard operating procedure called for GIs to fire first and ask questions later. Gore told a friend that he hated to see the U.S. debasing itself by carrying on an armed conflict rather than using civilized means of resolving problems.

During the conflict, Gore wrote friends in the States about his revulsion at seeing women and children cut in half by America's Huey helicopter gunships, and said that if he survived Vietnam, he was going to divinity school to "atone for my sins."

The reactions he described were those of many other Vietnam War veterans: revulsion at the sight of atrocities, a lingering horror and disillusionment, yet a strange urge to return to that scene of the most intense experience of his life. Along with his concern for human suffering there was a sense of shame because his country was debasing itself by waging that war.

While he was in Vietnam, Al Gore filed numerous stories from the combat zone. One of these stories, headlined "Fire Base Blue Is Overrun," was reprinted on 3/21/71 by *The Tennessean*:[20]

"Fire Base Blue Is Overrun"
By Sp. 5 Albert Gore Jr.

"Fire Support Base Blue (20th Engineers Brigade 10). 'Overrun' is a fairly explicit military term, but its full meaning is known only to those who live through it.

"It describes the most nitty-gritty conflict that a soldier ever sees. For that soldier, all the elaborate plans and maneuvers of the opposite armies fade momentarily into abstraction as the real nature of war is crystallized in a battle for his life.

"Survival depends on instantaneous reaction, and a good deal of courage. All of this was demonstrated brilliantly last week by the men of C Company, 31st Engineer Battalion (Combat), 20 Engineer Brigade, when Fire Support Base Blue was overrun.

"Fire Support Base Blue is a small compound near the Cambodian border in military Region III. Of the 135 people stationed there, only 35 are engineers. The others are artillerymen firing eight-inch guns into Cambodia, and 'duster' crews firing the twin 40mm. guns mounted on M52 tracked vehicles."
"Quick Response"

"The primary mission of the engineers is improving and maintaining the local road net, and building up gun pads. But when the attack began, it was the 35 engineers who responded quickly and effectively to save the fire base.

"On the night of February 22 there was no moon. The men sacked out early as usual, soon after the movie was over. 'Bloody Mama' with Shelley Winters as the maniac murderess. The guards were posted as usual. The password was fear.

"About nine o'clock the radar operator sent down a message that an unidentified group had moved to within 400 meters of the perimeter. But that wasn't out of the ordinary at all. That close to the border it happens more often than not. And as usual, they asked for permission to open fire with the dusters. 'Request denied,' there was an ARVN patrol in the area."

"OPENED UP"

"Three hours later, at 12:15, a trip flare was set off on the outside strand of barbed wire. The dusters immediately opened up and plastered the area. Then silence. Probably another rabbit—and probably a dead one by now.

"Those not on guard were lulled back to sleep by the deafening concussions of the eight-inch guns carrying out a night fire support mission.

"At 2:15 in the morning, there was an explosion that everybody heard. 'Incoming' "Hit the barn.'

"After the initial blast, many more followed in quick succession. As the men ran out of their hootches, one of the big guns was already in flames. 'All hell broke loose, man,' recalls SP4 Henry Akins III of Nashville, Tennessee.

"The CO, Lt. James M. Smith of Anderson, Indiana, was one of the first out—barefooted, wearing undershorts, a flak jacket, and a steel pot. He and the more experienced NCO's quickly took charge, 'Get the hell on the Barn!'

"They all had the same scenario in mind; this was a mortar barrage that probably would be followed by a ground attack. They were wrong. 'At first, I thought they were mortar,' says Smith, 'but it didn't sound the same, and the flashes were definitely different.'

"Staff Sergeant Preston E. Thompson of Yeager, W. Va., noticed the artillery bunkers were empty with two M60 machine-guns loaded and unguarded. His exact words can't properly be reproduced, but the tough veteran of Tet '68 didn't need to ponder the possibilities very long. He quickly put two engineers on each of the machine-guns."

"Solid Explosions"

"For the first fifteen minutes, there were solid explosions throughout the compound. Almost all the men were on the barn line with their weapons in ready for attack. The dusters were firing away at anything unlucky enough to be outside the perimeter.

"The explosions kept up. And they all seemed to be hits. The eight-inch was already gone, one of the dusters was now in flames, the sandbag bunker beside it was flattened, an entire row of hootches was destroyed. Either they were accurate shots, or. . .

"'VC in the compound! VC in the compound!' Suddenly everyone was yelling it. The dogs were barking it.

"Instead of panicking, the engineers coolly readjusted to the new situation. Staff Sergeant Leland F. Piper of Antigo, Wisc., another veteran of Tet '68, was checking out his men's positions at the time the cry went up. 'I just turned half of them around with their weapons pointed inside the compound.' The other NCO's were doing the same."

"Satchel Charges"

"Actually, the VC had been in the compound from the beginning. That first explosion was not a mortar but an RPG (rocket propelled grenade) that cut a large hole in the wire mesh directly in front of the eight-inch gun. Then a band of 20 Viet Cong 'zappers' (they zap people, they don't sap them) quickly slipping through the hole unseen and began throwing satchel charges all over the place.

"Probably the first man to see them was one of the duster crewchiefs. Immediately after the first explosion, several of them ran right by him while he was in the latrine. Since he was clad in his underwear and armed only with a flashlight, he sat tight until they left.

"They weren't seen by anyone else until 15 minutes later. There are several explanations why. First, as Lt. Smith says, 'They were good. They knew what they were doing.' Second, they apparently knew the exact location of their targets and didn't have to spend time searching the compound and take the chance of bumping into people. And third, their camouflage was exceptionally good. Wearing only shorts and small hats, they were covered from head to foot with charcoal. 'Even their eyelids,' remembers Sgt. Robert L. Simmins of Dayton, Ky. 'You couldn't see one if he was right next to you.'"

"Wrong Number"

"As soon as the word was out that the VC were inside, everybody started wondering who was next to him. SP4 William Curtis turned around to check the guy next to him and thought he recognized his walk. 'Gunman?' he asked just to make sure. Wrong number, GI. The VC was probably still wondering what 'Gunman' meant when he reached the other side of the compound.

"For the next half-hour there was a lot of confusion on both sides. One of the VC saw the shower tree out of the corner of his eye and riddled it with AK47 rounds. Many of the satchel charges were thrown with dead fuses. Seemingly, they were running around all over the place.

"One of them ran right smack dab into AP5 Donald McKenzie. During the struggle, the Zapper beat him over the head with the RPG he was carrying and ran away fast. 'Grandpops' McKenzie is now one of the few men who can claim he caught a direct hit on the head with an RPG and lived.

"The two seasoned veterans of the engineer group, Staff Sergeants Piper and Thompson, drew on their experience to deal with the situation. 'Usually you know where they're at,' says Piper. 'Here, you didn't know where they were.'

"Thompson, who was stationed at Fire Support Base Yeager when it was overrun in 1968, adds, 'You can't just sit there when you got VC in the compound. There's only one thing to do: that's find 'em and pin 'em down.'

"He and Lt. Smith got teams up to do just that. With most of the men left on the barn line, the teams set about searching the hootches, the bunkers, everywhere."

"A Live Round"

"In the process, they found a lot of other problems to be dealt with. The eight-inch gun, still burning, had a live round laying in the fire just behind the chamber. Thompson barked, 'Where is the crew to that gun?' Then, without waiting for an answer, he dispatched three engineers: Simmins, Curtis, and Sp4 Francis T. Christie of Linwood, Pa. to put out the fire.

"Christie was the first one on the gun. 'An AK started throwing rounds at us and I just hit the ground.' They got up and started hassling with the CO-2 extinguishers but they were empty. Finally, with more extinguishers, they brought the fire under control and moved the 250 pound shell before it could go off.

"Meanwhile, on the other end of the compound, one of the VC was attempting to escape. He ran down a row of hootches toward duster number four, still carrying a loaded rocket launcher. 'Max,' a large mongrel dog adopted by the Duster crew, met him halfway. Alerted by the barking, SPC Steve Vanderleit of Chicago looked up just in time to see the VC hurtling himself over the double row of barbed wire in a leap.

"'Max,' who looks for all the world like a small Siberian wolf, hurtled in right behind him. As soon as the VC hit the ground, Max caught him by the throat and brought him down. The VC managed to wrestle free, but one step and Max had him by the throat again.

"'I didn't want to shoot at first,' says Vanderleit, 'because Max was right there but as soon as the light hit them, Max just let go and moved away— like he knew what was going to happen.'

"It's entirely possible that Max did know. After all, he's been a 'duster dog' for five years. Originally, he belonged to another crew at Catum, but one day the battery commander ran by in a rush and Max brought him down.

"'That's why we're out here in the boonies,' says SP4 Christopher Blake, and 'I know for a fact that that dog saved somebody's life on this track; that zapper wasn't carrying RPGs for nothing.'

"Three more VC tried to escape by the mess hall 50 yards away, but they came in view of the nearby ARVN compound and were killed immediately.

"That might have been the last of them for all anyone knew. There was relative quiet in the compound except for the ammunition still blowing up duster number two. The other VC might have escaped unseen.

"DEAD and WOUNDED"

"But the engineer teams kept up the search. Inside the row of artillery hootches that had been destroyed, they found American dead and wounded, but no VC.

"The engineers' medic, SP4 Sylvester D. Thompson of Saginaw, Mich., had his hands full for the next several hours. The Medivac helicopters still hadn't arrived.

"In fact, the only helicopter that had reached the scene was the personal ship of Col. Leslie R. Forney Jr., deputy commander of the 23rd Artillery Group. He and his sergeant major, Charlie Thariac, left Long Binh the minute the radio operator woke them up, and landed under fire at 3:00 a.m.

"The search continued. Finally at 4:30 a.m. Sgt. Piper peered into the storage bunker where the artillery shells are kept and saw 'two maybe as many as five VC.' He asked them to surrender. They didn't.

"SP4 Akins recalls, 'That Piper, he doesn't fear anything. He walked right around the corner and said, 'Lai day' (Come here).' The nearest one to him raised his hands and gave a slight sidelong glance over his shoulder.

"Following his eyes, Piper saw another VC rising out of the darkness with something in his hands. Piper jumped backwards just before a satchel charge blew a hole in the concrete floor he had been standing on. It was followed by a grenade. Still wearing only one boot, Piper tried to kick it away, but luckily it was a dud.

"So much for Lai Day and Chiey Hoi and all that. Within 20 seconds of the blast, Lt. Smith had his men placed completely around the storage bunker. Just as the circle closed the VC decided to run for it.

"NO DICE"

"Un-nh, no dice. Sgt. Thompson exchanged rounds with one of them at point blank range for a while, and the VC changed their minds and backed into the bunker again.

"'We didn't know it at the time,' says Piper,'but they were out of grenades and only had one AK47.' There were other complications too. First of all it was still pitch dark. Simmins was setting off flares at 10 second intervals. 'I was waiting two or three seconds between each one, sort of hoping they would try to make a break and then catch 'em in the open with the next burst.'

"The main problem, though, was the bunker itself. Many of the artillery shells inside were armed and ready to go off. Even worse, there was a large stack of cylinders inside filled with pure cordite, the highly explosive powder used to propel 250 pound shells 37 miles. In short, there was enough cordite to make Fire Base Blue nothing but a big hole in the ground.

"So they decided to wait until daylight.

"Two hours later, at the break of dawn, Simmins had only two flares left. About 7:00 a.m., a group of 1st Cavalry advisors arrived from the nearby ARVN compound and advised throwing a few grenades into the bunker. They didn't take the advice.

"When it was sufficiently light, Col. Forney walked up and tossed a grenade of CS inside, and within minutes, four VC came staggering out with their hands over their faces.

"The 1st Cavalry interpreter learned from them that they had come from Cambodia to knock out the fire base because several days before one of its guns had scored a direct hit on a secret VC hospital.

"The interpreter also learned that inside the bunker there was another VC dead. The engineers made the prisoners bring his body out—just in cast it was booby-trapped. Then they went inside themselves and found the artillery canisters pried open and a large pile of cordite on the floor.

"Five Were Dead"

"Relieved, the engineers set about the job of cleaning up and caring for any remaining wounded. 'Doc' Thompson, conscientious objector, had been patching up serious cases all night. He had seen 23 men medivacked and five dead. Now he was caring for the wounded VC.

"There was a lot of work to be done. Sgt. Thompson, after finding out that no EOD (explosive ordnance disposal) teams were available, organized engineer teams to do it themselves.

"They found 30 satchel charges that hadn't gone off and exploded them in a safe place. In the latrine, they found a flashlight boobytrapped with grenades. Other engineers buried the VC dead behind the gasoline storage tank. Still others set about cleaning up the debris that used to be hootches or bunkers.

"Later in the day they stopped work for an award ceremony. Brigadier General K.B. Cooper, commanding general of the 20th Engineering Brigade, awarded four Bronze Stars on the spot: to Staff Sergeants Thompson and Piper, Sgt. Simmins, and SP5 Christie. And more medals are in the works.

"'The trouble with putting these guys in for medals,' says Lt. Smith, 'is that you're supposed to pick out one act of heroism that the award is for. It just wasn't like that, these guys did it all night long.' He might have included himself; SP4 Akins says, 'He's got it together and men know it. Now, when he says jump, we ask how high on the way up.'

"'It's great when you do the job, come through with flying colors, and have few hurt,' says Smith, 'but I guess no amount of practice or having it up tight can match dumb luck.'

"Maybe, but the Engineers came through the conflict with only three minor injuries and no fatalities. Most of the dead and wounded were hit either in the first series of blasts, or were caught in their hootches.

"That night at dinner, there was a strong spirit, and too many war stories. Then someone brought in an intelligence report that one of the fire bases in the area was going to be overrun on the night of February 22nd.

"'Oh yeah? No kidding?'"

*   *   *

Finally, the Vietnam nightmare ended, and Al Gore Jr., different from the young man who had flown in to Vietnam just months earlier, boarded a plane to return to Carthage.

Edd Blair (1988)

Al Gore Jr. and constituent (1976)

Al, Karenna, Tipper and Kristin (1978; photo by Jack Gunter, courtesy *Nashville Banner*)

Al and Tipper (photo by Bob Ray, courtesy *Nashville Banner*)

Jerry Futrell

Chapter Six

I have used the words "the qualities of youth." Be wise enough, be tolerant enough, you who are young in years, to remember that millions of older people have kept and propose to keep these qualities of youth. You ought to thank God tonight, if, regardless of your dreams, you are young enough in spirit to dream dreams and see visions—dreams and visions about a greater and finer America that is to be----Hold fast to your dream. America needs it.

Franklin Delano Roosevelt
Speech at Baltimore, Maryland, April 13, 1936. Public Papers, V. 166

The bands weren't playing and there weren't any parades awaiting returning Vietnam GIs in Smith County or in Washington when Al Gore Jr. returned in May 1971. Sad at heart and troubled to the depths of his soul, Gore needed healing, and he sought it among friends and in the place that he had loved the most growing up—Tennessee. He brought Tipper to Tennessee with him, and soon she too was enchanted by the beauty of the region, the rich farm land and the rolling hills that surround the Caney Fork and Cumberland Rivers that snake through the hollows of Middle Tennessee near Carthage.

It was obvious to his old friends that he was changed, at loose ends, unsure about himself, his future, but positive at the time that the last thing he wanted was a career in politics.

Donna Rankin recalls a different Al Gore after Vietnam. "He didn't know what he wanted to do when he came back," she said. "The war must have been horrible."

Tennessee Highway Patrol Sergeant Edd Blair believes any president who orders troops into combat "ought to have seen what war is really all about." "Al came back," he says, "even more serious than he was before. And lots of people who don't know him think he's too serious. I was

Dalton Minchey stands before his home in Tanglewood subdivision, the first home built by Al Gore and his partners.

with him pretty often when he moved back and worked at *The Tennessean.* He was trying to get some things settled in his mind."

Disillusioned by the treatment his father had received six months earlier at the hands of Tennessee voters when they had rejected his Senate re-election try, Al Gore resisted the senior Gore's not-so-veiled efforts to interest him in local politics. Early on, his father had wanted him to follow both his parents by going to law school.

Bill Kovach, editor of the *Atlanta Constitution,* recalled in an interview by Chattanooga reporter Dick Kopper in 1985 that the elder Gore strongly disagreed with Al's decision to become a reporter with *The Tennessean.* Kovach said the elder Gore even asked Kovach, who had known young Gore since meeting him at the 1964 Democratic National Convention, to intervene. "At the request of his father," Kovach said, "I tried to talk him out of going into the newspaper business. I urged him to go to law school. He could always be a newspaper reporter, but he couldn't always go to law school. He should take advantage of the opportunity."[1]

"And he was smart enough to ignore my advice and do both," Kovach added with a laugh.[2]

There was no question Gore was quieter, more reflective. Tipper remembers that she would wake in the night, find him out on the farm, walking around, unable to sleep, deeply troubled by his Vietnam experiences. He talked about "atonement for things he saw and did in

Vietnam.'He put out a garden, worked around the farm, all the while introducing Tipper to life in a small Southern town.³

Although he'd always loved life on the farm, he found a special therapy in working in the soil during that time. As a young boy he often expressed amazement at the miracle of life, by planting seeds in the black, pulverized soil they worked just to the right consistency, and then seeing life spring forth. He watched that miracle in the spring and summer of 1971, and making peace with nature did wonders for his soul.

He worked with Walter King Robinson, his partner in Tanglewood Home Builders Inc., in the development and building that was going on at the Tanglewood Subdivision, which was shaping up nicely.

Dalton Minchey is the Gulf dealer on Main Street in Carthage. He and his wife live on Highway 25 in the Tanglewood Subdivision, in the first house Al Gore and his partners built years ago. "Yes," he said, looking up from a dirty engine, wiping oil from a dipstick. "I'll talk to you about Al Gore and the house I live in. It's a good house and I'm proud of it. I like the house and I like young Al. Known him and his family for years. Fine folks."

"The working man needs political leaders like Al Gore. I'm for him, so's my family. I just wish everybody could know Al and his folks like we do here in Carthage," he said, tugging at a stubborn windshield wiper insert. "I just wish somebody else would build some more houses that good and that affordable in this day and time."

The Tennessee Secretary of State in Nashville keeps the records of businesses which incorporate under the laws of Tennessee. Tanglewood Home Builders, Inc., 207 N. Main Street, Carthage, Tennessee 37030, had a good record on file during its operation from September 18, 1969, until 1981. According to documents filed by the Tanglewood Board of Directors, made up of President Albert Gore Jr., Secretary-Treasurer Walter K. Robinson, and Albert Gore, the purpose of the corporation was "to develop real estate holdings and construct buildings for sale."

"Al Gore is like family to me," said Walter King Robinson Jr. of Carthage, who was Gore's partner in Tanglewood Home Builders and who would later become his first campaign manager. "Al and I and his daddy put together the company, and built houses together when Al came home from service."

Robinson said he'd been interviewed by reporters who attempted to downplay young Gore's participation in the business. "I enjoyed working with him, and I'm proud of our association and the little subdivision we developed out there on Highway 25, on land that in years past had once been owned by my family," he said.

Robinson described his youthful partner as serious minded, even as a youth. "He puts everything he has into every effort he makes," recalled

Vanderbilt Divinity School

The Tennessean building, 1100 Broadway, Nashville

Robinson, "basically because he wants to do a good job with anything he's connected with. He's a fine young man, whose character and integrity will carry him to the presidency someday. He gives 100% in friendship, loyalty, and effort, and I'm proud of him, his intelligence, and accomplishments."

In the fall of 1971, Al Gore enrolled for graduate work at the Vanderbilt University School of Divinity in Nashville, about a sixty-mile drive from the farm. His course work centered on philosophy and phenomenology, as he tried to work through "the spiritual issues that were most important to me at the time." He says of that time: "I was interested in a structured opportunity to explore the most important questions that I had in my life. . . . And it was one of the most valuable years I've ever spent. I found a lot better questions."[4]

Dr. Walter Harrelson was the dean and Dr. Herman Norton and Dr. Eugene TeSelle were professors at the Divinity School during Al Gore's two years there in the early 1970's. All recalled him very favorably as a student.

"I had him in my Religion and Natural Sciences course," Dr. TeSelle said. "He was a good and motivated student, highly intelligent, alert, and attentive. He talked about his parents, I recall, who were from different churches, and once said something about having 'a foot in both churches,' though I don't recall the churches he mentioned. He was well adjusted, highly respected by the faculty, and an impressive young man."

If Al Gore had really sought to avoid service in Vietnam, he could have done so easily by enrolling in divinity school prior to military service instead of afterwards. Those who foresaw a bright political future for the young farmer-builder were delighted he attended divinity school after he had served in Vietnam, not before.

Even with the added work and stimulation he found in graduate school, Gore had still not found himself, although he was certain that he would never be drawn into a political career. He'd enjoyed his work as a journalist in the Army, and thought newspaper work might be his calling. Since the *Nashville Tennessean* had always supported his father, and since he knew many of its reporters, he asked then-editor John Seigenthaler for a job as a reporter on the night shift. Seigenthaler, impressed with the story Gore had filed from Vietnam, sent him to city editor Frank Ritter for a formal job interview.

Frank Ritter, now deputy managing editor of *The Tennessean,* says he is sure that Wayne Whitt and at least one other *Tennessean* executive also interviewed and passed on Gore before he was hired. "Gore," Ritter recalled, "worked long hours. He wanted to be a success as a writer, a new discipline for him. He had everything it took to be an outstanding journalist."

"He did it all as a cub reporter," Ritter said. "Police beat, obituaries, local school news, but he was innovative. We were trying to come up with a new approach to coverage of the Nashville Christmas parade, an event that's been held for over forty years, and were stumped. Al came up with the idea of writing the piece through the eyes of Ebenezer Scrooge and Tiny Tim, and a fine piece resulted, something very characteristic of his work."

After Gore announced for the presidency in April 1987, Frank Ritter wrote about Gore's employment at the paper in an article headlined "Gore knows well his priorities":[5]

"When we at *The Tennessean* interview job candidates, frequently questions take the form of a scenario; the applicant is asked to say how he or she would respond to a situation.

"When I interview, I ask: 'What would you do if your editor ordered you to write a story with which you disagreed, or knew to be false?'

"No matter what the job candidate answers, I'm lying in wait with the next question. If the answer is, 'I would have to follow my editor's orders,' then I ask: 'You mean you're willing to violate your conscience — to have your name over a story you know to be a lie?' If the answer is, 'I couldn't agree to write an untruth,' then I ask: 'You mean you would be the kind of employee who would refuse to follow your editor's directions?'

"What I'm looking for, of course, is not necessarily the answer to my first question, although I am, indeed, interested in whether the applicant has integrity; instead, I'm trying to see how he reacts under pressure.

"A lot of people wilt under questioning. They are so concerned with trying to figure out the answer they think I'm looking for, that they fail to look inside themselves to see how they truly think and feel.

"Albert Gore Jr. was not among those who wilted. When I interviewed him in the fall of 1971 for a job as reporter for *The Tennessean,* it was the first time I had met him. I tried my best to intimidate him, rattle him, confuse him, trip him up, make him vacillate.

"I was not successful. Al had a sure sense of self. He refused to be intimated, and he didn't back up. When I asked, 'What would you do if your editor ordered you to write a story you knew to be untrue?' he answered immediately.

"'I can't imagine that an editor would ever ask a reporter to do that. It would be unprofessional. But if it happened, I would resign before I violated my conscience.'

"It was the best answer I've ever gotten to that question.

"Al got the job and soon was immersed in covering such weighty things as Madison's Hillbilly Day, the firing of a Metro fireman for having long hair, burglaries, tavern brawls, and the local Veteran's Day parade.

"He advanced to other assignments—city government, investigative reporting, politics. He was a reporter for three years, then took a year's leave of absence and returned as an editorial writer before resigning in 1976 to run for Congress.

"Al was not, initially, the best writer I'd ever seen. In fact, he was awfully green. In those ancient days, we still used typewriters; and Al's messy copy resembled nothing so much as hen scratching where he had penciled in numerous corrections and additions.

"And he was awfully slow at first. 'Al, we gotta have that story now!' became a familiar refrain in *The Tennessean* cityroom as deadline neared.

"But Al excelled in many ways. He was a reporter's reporter. If he was late with his copy, frequently it was because he hated to stop digging and asking questions. He had those characteristics of curiosity and aggressiveness that you can't teach. You can teach writing—and Al soon learned to write very well, and to meet his deadlines—but you can't teach initiative and integrity. Fortunately, Al didn't need instructions in those areas.

"He would have made a great journalist. But he gave up that noblest of professions to enter the political arena. And what I remember most about that switch was that immediately upon announcing his candidacy for Congress he stopped parting his hair in the middle and began to part it on the right side. He also began wearing suits.

"After that, we would hear from Al frequently. Most often, he served as his own press secretary, calling the city editor to say, 'Tonight at my public meeting, I plan to announce. . . .' He knew what was news, and he knew how to make news. He knew what would make a good 'lead,' and he knew the value of good quotes. He made things easy for editors and reporters.

"Sometimes he would drop by the office late at night, after a long day of travel in his district, to pick up a newspaper. We sometimes would talk politics then—for example, I wanted to know why he didn't agree with me about gun control—but more often the talk centered around personal things.

"I wanted to know how his home life was going. How was it possible to spend all that time on the road and still meet his responsibilities to his wife and children? Did he see Tipper enough? Did he have time to parent? Did he still jog?

"What I feared was that my friend and former colleague would lose balance. In pursuit of his political career, he might neglect the more important things in life—namely, his family and health. But he seemed always to have his head on straight. He was aware of the problems, he said, and he would not sacrifice his family life.

"One time, he became overweight and confessed, 'I've not been running and exercising as I should.' Next time I saw him, which was a few weeks later, he had lost all the extra weight. 'I just stopped eating and started running,' he confided.

"Now, Al is running again—this time for president. His resolve to meet his first responsibility—to his wife and children—will be sorely tested. He wants to be president, and I want that for him, but there are more important things than being president.

"Al knows all this already. But I'm betting that the same sense of self and confidence will ensure that he will have both—the presidency *and* the family life that has sustained him so well."

Jim O'Hara's desk was near Gore's when they were both fledgling reporters with *The Tennessean* in the early 1970's, and he covered his old colleague during much of the 1987-88 campaign. He recalled that as a beginning reporter, Gore thrived on pressure, even when the pressure was on in a case involving corruption of two councilmen. "He was extremely tenacious. He hated mistakes," O'Hara recalled. "Al was a careful reporter, somebody who wanted to take the time he knew was necessary to a story. Needless to say, on a daily newspaper, that drove editors up the wall."

"He was always pushing, always trying to ask the tough questions.

His desk was generally messy, but his mind was clear."

Another newspaperman who can speak of Al Gore as a colleague is Jerry Thompson. Thompson has been with *The Tennessean* since the early 1960's, rising from cub reporter through the ranks until he's now a featured columnist. He once spent fifteen months infiltrating the Ku Klux Klan, and later wrote a book about his Klan experiences. He's had the experiences to judge character and ability, and he rates Gore at the top. He met Gore during the younger man's first days on the job.

"Since I'm going to be covering your old beat at the police department each night, how about taking me over and introducing me around?" Gore asked him.

"Sure," Thompson replied, looking at the young reporter he thought to be independently wealthy. Thompson was glad to help him, because he thought the Senator's son probably had a slick new Mercedes or at least a Cadillac parked nearby in two parking spots to avoid nicks or scrapes in the paint.

They went outside the building and Gore stopped at the dirtiest, roughest-looking, most banged-up old Chevrolet Thompson had ever seen. "This is it," said Gore, climbing in, as he motioned for Thompson to get in. Thompson thought it was a joke, perhaps.

Gore had to try the engine several times before it caught, and as they left, the old car sputtered and coughed. By this time Thompson had abandoned any thought of impressing his police buddies; now he was hoping none of his friends at the station would see him rolling up in Gore's old car.

Lost in thought, Thompson paid little attention to the police unit which pulled alongside, signaling Gore to the curb. Gore jumped out to find out what was wrong, but Thompson eased down in the seat, hoping the two patrol officers wouldn't recognize him.

"What's the trouble, Officer?" Gore asked.

"One of your headlights isn't working," the officer replied. Thompson expected that Gore would tell him he was a reporter, would have the light repaired as soon as possible, and that they'd be on their way.

Gore looked at the officer as if he didn't understand what was happening, then suddenly ran to the front of the car. As the officer looked on, amazed, Gore delivered a hefty kick to the offending headlight.

As if by magic, a beam of light shot from the headlight he'd just kicked. The beam, however, was not aimed toward the front of the car, but shone onto the side of a building to the left of where they were parked.

As the officer started to speak, Gore kicked the headlight again, locking it into the proper position. The beam could not have been better positioned.

Gore's apartment residence,
West End Avenue, Nashville

Rental home at 1113 Belvedere
Dr., Nashville

The officer stood, silent, dumbfounded.

Gore stared a moment at him, then said, "That's all right, Officer, it does that all the time." With that, the officer shook his head and returned to his unit. Gore smiled all the way to the station.

Wayne Whitt is the managing editor of *The Tennessean*. He says Al Gore's an extrovert, a man of conviction, knows the newspaper business and how to grab headlines. "I never thought he'd stay here. . . . Aggressive, liked to pursue political corruption."

"I was surprised at the pot business," Whitt said. "I never saw any indication of that around here."

* * *

During his first weeks as a night reporter at the paper, Gore commuted from Carthage, but the sixty-mile one-way trip became too much. He approached Alex Wade, a well-known and respected insurance agency owner in Nashville, about a small apartment in a building on busy West End Avenue that owner Wade had advertised for rent.

"The place was pretty bad," Wade recalls, "but Gore never complained. That's the thing that struck me. He never thought he was too good for the place, which was basically just a room with a bed, hotplate and bathroom. It didn't even have a kitchen."

Wade said the other tenants complained a great deal about the noise

Tipper photographs daughters Kristin and Sarah

the heating system made, but he never heard a word of complaint from Gore. "He paid his rent, sixty-five dollars a month, promptly, and was the best tenant I had there," said Wade. "It finally became such a hassle we sold the building."

After he gave up the small flat he had rented from Wade, Gore rented a room from two of his colleagues at *The Tennessean,* reporters John C. and Nancy Warnecke. They had a small house on a quiet street near David Lipscomb College, where his sister had attended high school during the 1951-52 year.

Bernie Arnold has lived across from the little house at 1113 Belvedere Drive for over thirty years but doesn't remember the Gores' living there. "It's a small house that's been rented through the years, but I would have recalled if there had been anything unusual there. I have known and admired the Gore family for years, but didn't realize Al and Tipper once lived across the street," she said. "I'm going to call everyone I know and tell them."

To occupy herself while Al worked each night, Tipper enrolled in a night course in photography at Nashville Tech. After Jack Corn, the class instructor, saw her potential, he offered her a job at *The Tennessean,* where he was chief photographer. She then began working several days in the photo lab and took pictorial assignments for the paper.

Before the Gore children were born, Tipper began graduate study in psychology at George Peabody College, where she received her master's degree several years later.

* * *

Gore threw himself wholeheartedly into his career at the newspaper, working long hours, doggedly pursuing investigative leads, sometimes working through the night. He had served his apprenticeship well, covering local news events, parades, musicals, bus rides, hamburger eating contests and the night police beat. In 1973 he was rewarded with an advancement to a coveted assignment: part-time coverage at the State Capitol and the Davidson County Courthouse, which houses Nashville's courts and its Metropolitan Council.

"He loved working at *The Tennessean*," Tipper has said in numerous interviews. "He was as enthusiastic about the police beat as he was about the Metro beat."

In 1973, amidst a flurry of rumors of widespread corruption, Gore became involved in at least two investigations, both involving alleged payoffs to members of the Metro Council. A businessman who had just completed a tour of duty as grand jury foreman sought Gore out and told him that a building project he was involved in with several partners had been brought to a standstill because the Metro councilman in the district had refused to sponsor an alley-closing ordinance unless paid to do so. Since it appeared to Gore that this was a criminal matter, District Attorney Tom Shriver was brought into the case. In the investigation which followed, Gore was present when the informant was wired for sound by state investigators, and then participated in the surveillance of the meet to discuss the payoff. Gore heard the councilman say that he wanted "a grand" ($1,000) to have the Metro Council close the alley.

Frank Empson, now head of *The Tennessean*'s photography department, was a staff photographer in 1973, shooting pictures for general assignment. After Gore had done the leg work on the alley-closing investigation and taken the case to *Tennessean* executives and state police, editor John Seigenthaler assigned Empson to join a three-man photographic team to record a payoff to the councilman.

"I remember how excited he became when he had the chance to nail a crooked politician," Empson said of Al Gore Jr. "The day of the payoff, Jack Corn, Bill Preston and I took our cameras into Bill Willis' law office at Seventh and Union. From there we could see the front of the Downtowner Motel, where the meet was to take place.

"Al, John Seigenthaler, some TBI agents and the lawyer whose office we were in watched, too. The councilman drove up in his car, the businessman who was cooperating with Al went to the car, and we shot pictures of the councilman taking the envelope with the money. I used my Nikon with a 200 mm lens. The businessman had a recorder on, so the tape and our pictures were a big part of the evidence.

"Al did a great job," the veteran photographer said. "He had everything it took to be a great journalist. But he was very disappointed when the trial resulted in a mistrial, and lots of folks around here think that's why he decided to go on to law school."

While this case was being investigated, Gore also covered the probe of another councilman who was indicted for allegedly taking a $2,500 payoff to sponsor legislation affecting a shopping center in his district. In the prosecutive action and trials which followed and which Gore covered, he saw the American judicial and criminal justice system at work for the first time. He found it difficult to sit in the courtroom and hear the evidence questioned, especially since he'd been there, had seen and heard the events as they occurred.

When the judge declared a mistrial in the first case, Gore sat in the courtroom, shocked, and has since told his colleagues and numerous interviewers that he made an instantaneous decision that he would enroll in law school, because "I needed to learn more about a legal system that would allow this." In the other case, though the councilman was convicted and sentenced to a prison term, he never served a day.

As Gore continued to cover the Metro Council and occasionally sessions of the Tennessee General Assembly, he grew more frustrated and tired with the process of seeing wrong decisions made and then, in his position as a reporter, being able only to report them accurately and fairly with the hope that the general public would see the mistakes as well. And as he heard the debate, he began to feel that perhaps he should be involved, more than just writing about it. He began to feel a certain amount of frustration when the debate went in a direction that seemed to be clearly wrong.

More significantly, Gore saw that his own capabilities qualified him to compete with the legislators and councilpersons he'd covered. Increasingly frustrated with the limitations of journalism, he was being drawn by his own competitive spirit closer and closer to becoming a participant. He was slowly being drawn into politics, the profession he had rejected.

*   *   *

In 1974, Gore took a leave of absence from *The Tennessean,* dropped out of Vanderbilt's divinity school and transferred to its law school, where his mother had been the second woman to graduate in 1936.

His father was secretly delighted with the move. The senior Gore said, "He said to me, 'I have decided that the law is the cutting edge of our

Rental duplex at 1114 Morrow
Ave., Nashville

Gore home at 4421 Sheppard
Pl., Nashville

society,' and I said, 'Well, did you find the answers to those troublesome questions?'"

"He smiled and said, 'Well, at least I've learned to ask more intelligent questions.'"[6]

Dr. Paul Hartman has been a professor at the Vanderbilt Law School since 1949, and recalls Al Gore's attendance. "He didn't graduate because he had an opportunity to run for the House," Dr. Hartman said, "but he was an impressive and fine young man who would have made an outstanding lawyer, I think. His enrollment was completely favorable, and any book bearing his name relating to leadership is appropriate."

Karenna, the young couple's first child, was born in Nashville on August 6, 1973. Six weeks later, Al and Tipper bought a farm and house in the Elmwood community from his parents for $80,000, according to the deed filed at the register's office in Carthage. Consisting of approximately eighty rolling acres of mostly pastureland and an attractive 2,100-square-foot ranch brick home, the property is directly across the Caney Fork River from the senior Gores' farm.

Al and Tipper, now attending schools and working in Nashville, moved into one side of a newly constructed duplex at 1114 Morrow Drive. Since this house was only about two hundred yards from their Belvedere Drive home, they were able to keep their old telephone number. They remained in this modest, quiet neighborhood behind a landmark in the area, Hutcherson's Pharmacy, until January 14, 1975, when they purchased their first home in Nashville, at 4421 Sheppard Place.

The home was attractively built of brownstone and trimmed in brown, and was situated on nearly an acre in an older, established neighborhood. According to the register of deeds in Davidson County, Al and Tipper purchased the property for $76,000, financed through the Citizens Bank of Carthage.

From all outward appearances in 1975, Al and Tipper Gore had established themselves for life in Nashville. They had purchased a residence, had a child, and were both engaged in challenging careers at *The Tennessean*. Though Tipper was in the last phase of her graduate program at Peabody College, she was spending more and more of her time carrying out photographic duties at the paper. With slightly more than a year left at Vanderbilt Law School, which he attended mornings and early afternoons, Al Gore was rapidly on his way to becoming an editorial writer of national prominence at *The Tennessean,* where he worked nights.

Gore's boss in the editorial section, Lloyd Armour, now retired, rates him as an excellent journalist, one with a brilliant career in the field had he continued.

Tennessean publisher John Seigenthaler said, "He was a terrific reporter. He had all the right instincts, all the right skills."

Even with this background and set of circumstances, however, Gore was like a firehorse waiting for the right call. Brilliant future in journalism and two years invested at Vanderbilt Law School notwithstanding, Gore was still unfulfilled, psychologically ready for the first call that would place him in a position of public service. He had come to understand, though not to agree with, the treatment his father had received when his long-time Tennessee constituents removed him from office in 1970. And, like many investigators who delve into corruption of public officials, he had developed a severe distaste for those who misused or forgot their public trust.

It was in late February 1976 that he received the call that would change his life forever.

*   *   *

"This is John, Al," Seigenthaler said. "Joe Evins is going to announce his retirement from Congress tomorrow. The story just came across my desk."

Gore thanked him and hung up. He had just gotten home from school and was about to leave for work, when the implication of John Seigenthaler's message hit him. Representative Joe L. Evins, a Smithville native who had represented Gore's district in Carthage for thirty years,

Al and Tipper's farm in Smith County, TN

had decided to give up his seat in Congress and not seek re-election from Tennessee's Fourth District.

Gore related to David Frost the details of how he'd come to run for Representative Evins' seat and confided: "I started doing pushups to start getting in physical shape for the contest, and I surprised myself with the extent to which I had come back to this feeling that I would try a career in public service. I didn't realize myself I had been pulled back so much to it."[7]

Around midnight Gore called his father, who was in California, and told him he was running for Congress.

"Dad, I've got a chance at your old seat in Congress, the Fourth Congressional District seat up home at Carthage. What do you think?" he asked.

Albert Gore Sr. said his son's unexpected action almost took his breath away, but after a moment of hesitation he finally responded to his son's question.

"Well, son, I'll vote for you," he said. The elder Gore maintains that was the extent of consultation he had in Al's decision to run.[8]

Al Gore Jr. continued, "But when I got into it, three days later I made my first speech—I'd made other speeches before, but not a real political speech. I walked out on the courthouse steps and made my first real speech announcing for Congress, and I walked down the street shaking hands with the first person I saw asking for their vote, and delivered the most awkward request for a vote you ever heard—it was tortured—

Tipper and Karenna watch as Al announces for Congress, 1976

but the next was easier and better, and by the tenth or twelfth time 'I was in the groove.'[9]

After Al announced that he was running, Tipper told her supervisor, Jack Corn, at the *Tennessean* photography lab, and asked for two or three days off each week to campaign with her husband. Amused at her political naivete, Corn laughed, then said, 'Tipper, your job will be here if Al loses, which he won't do. You need to get out there with him and campaign full time.'

That was all she needed to stir her into action. They listed their newly purchased home in Nashville for sale, then moved back to their farm at Carthage, where they planned campaign strategy.

To win the Fourth District Congressional seat that his father had held from 1939 to 1953, Gore had to win over eight other candidates in the Democratic Primary, which was tantamount to election because there was no Republican opposition to speak of.

Gore began a campaign that had overtones of those his father had run in the past, calling for more public jobs, higher taxes for the rich, support for the TVA, and more stringent strip-mine laws. He quickly became the front-runner in the race, largely because of name recognition and because there were no real issues in the race except the relative attractiveness of the candidates, an area in which Gore excelled. His principal opponent, state house majority leader Stanley Rogers, stressing his own experience, tried unsuccessfully to stir up debate over the young Gore's inexperience and youth.

Al asks farmers for their votes (courtesy *Nashville Banner*)

When Rogers' strategy failed, he tried to inject Gore's stated net worth of $273,000 as an issue. At the same time, he claimed that Gore's father, then chairman of the Island Creek Coal Company of Lexington, Kentucky, was tied to energy interests, not a very big secret in Smith County anyway.

From the beginning of this, his first campaign, Gore began a practice in dress that he has generally followed in subsequent campaigns. He always wore a dark blue suit and red tie and unshined shoes. Sometimes with Tipper with him, or Nancy, or his mother, he scouted the hills of Smith County and the other counties of the Fourth District, looking for votes. According to Smith Countians, he got better each time he spoke, talking openly about how he felt and honestly expressing his views.

When it was over, Gore had received 3,559 more votes than Rogers.

And in the general election that followed, Gore won easily over William H. McGlamery, who ran as an independent.

During the campaign Al and Tipper received an offer of $96,000 for their home on Sheppard Place. They closed the sale December 29, 1976.

Indeed, Al Gore had seized the moment when the call came in February, and now he and Tipper were about to embark on a political career at which experts still marvel.

Al, Davidson County Sheriff Fate Thomas, and Jim Sasser (1984; photo by Dave Findley, courtesy *Nashville Banner*)

Al and former Nashville Mayor Richard Fulton (photo by Dave Findley, courtesy *Nashville Banner*)

(photo by Jack Gunter, courtesy *Nashville Banner*)

Mr. and Mrs. William Thompson

Bonnie McKinney serves one of Al Gore's favorite meals as a youth.

Chapter Seven

The care of human life and happiness, not their destruction, is the first and only legitimate object of good government.

Thomas Jefferson
March 31, 1809

Speaker Tip O'Neil, Al, and Jim Sasser (photo by Dean Dixon, courtesy the *Nashville Banner*)

When Tipper's family in Arlington, Virginia, received word that Al had won and would be moving to the Washington area to take his father's

Rep. Al Gore Jr. arrives home in Arlington after a day on Capitol Hill
(photo by Jack Gunter, courtesy *Nashville Banner*)

old seat in the House of Representatives, there was an immediate air
of excitement in the Carlson home. Tipper's mother and grandmother,
Margaret and Verda, began preparations for the arrival of Tipper, Al
and Karenna (then three years old). And, of course, the senior Gores
had an apartment in Washington and were thrilled by the young family's
coming to the area.

At twenty-eight, Gore became one of the youngest Congressmen
elected from Tennessee in this century. When he was sworn in as a new
member of the House in January 1977, the man he was replacing, thirty-
two-year veteran Joe L. Evins Jr., known affectionately as "the Dean
of the House," introduced Gore to the House and the gallery, where
Al's and Tipper's families watched admiringly. Congressman Evins spoke

Rep. Gore in his office

glowingly of the freshman representative and predicted a bright future for him in Congress.

In accordance with a long-standing House tradition, Gore, an incoming rookie congressman, was assigned Room 1725 in the Longworth House Office Building, a small office with Spartan furnishings. His first assignments were to the House Committee on Interstate and Foreign Commerce and to the Committee on Science and Technology, both of which had jurisdiction over energy-related legislation.

Gore, unwilling to lose contact with constituents and supporters, began conducting open meetings throughout his district. His usual schedule called for him to work on Capitol Hill Monday to Friday, then dash to National Airport for a flight to Tennessee, and then hold several neighborhood meetings in his congressional district.

A typical meeting lasted approximately an hour; he prepared for each meeting, however, by checking his computer bank for names of persons who would probably attend, problems that might arise, constituency service requests and their status, and any information that might enhance his knowledge of the group or the location in which he was appearing. These meetings were carried out in keeping with Gore's demeanor as a serious legislator eager to serve his constituents. Normally, he solicited input from those who attended by asking for questions, then the dialogue flowed, as Gore told his people what the Congress was about and what the impact of its actions would be on them as citizens of Tennessee.

Always prepared, he answered questions ranging from defense to farm policy to Social Security. Never rude, Gore was patient and considerate, never hurrying anyone who wanted to speak.

And, as many of the ladies who attended say, "He's easy to look at, too."

In his early congressional days, before Nashville had its American Airlines hub, Gore nearly always flew back to Washington from Nashville on Sunday mornings. In 1987 American Airlines established a hub in Nashville, creating more flights to and from Washington to choose from, so he's now able to keep a more flexible schedule.

Before the 1987 campaign, he normally returned on Sundays to Washington's National Airport in time to rush home, pick up his family and attend worship services at nearby Mount Vernon Baptist Church. From the time the children were old enough to accompany them, Al and Tipper have tried to take them to art museums or symphonies at least twice a month. This Sunday afternoon activity is eagerly anticipated.

In their earliest years in Congress, the Gores had little time for social life, although occasionally they entertained colleagues at home, usually with a simple meal and pleasant conversation about anything but work.

Generally, he worked all the time. "It does make it a little difficult to have a social life," Tipper told a reporter at that time. "The usual social nights are Friday and Saturday and Al's out of town those nights. But I'm pretty self-reliant when he's gone. I take over and do things with the children, and then we all try to do something on Sunday when Al gets home."[1]

Gore occasionally plays tennis. He tries to reserve at least two hours each night with the children before they go to bed. Since the Gores have opted for a simpler life, they do occasionally have cookouts with the neighbors and evenings with the children. "Time with your family is just so precious," Gore has said. "I'd just rather be with them."

With his friendly nature and ready smile, Gore became popular with House members, particularly with fellow House novices Peter Kostmayer of Pennsylvania, David Bonior of Michigan and John

Mt. Vernon Baptist Church, Arlington, VA

Cavanaugh of Nebraska and committee colleagues like Phil Sharp of Indiana.

On June 5, 1977, the Gores had their second daughter, Kristin.

In 1978 he ran unopposed and was re-elected without opposition. He continued his back-breaking regimen of flying to Tennessee on the weekends for his neighborhood meetings.

On January 7, 1979, they had a third daughter, Sarah.

On March 19, 1979, Representative Albert Gore Jr. became the first House member to speak in front of TV cameras set to carry floor proceedings of the chamber.

In the next election, his third, in 1980, he received seventy-nine percent of the vote–137,612 votes to his opponent's 35,954–and won re-election to a third term over Republican James Beau Seigneur.

In 1982, while they were expecting their fourth child, discussions began about continuing the name Albert Arnold. Both were initially opposed to the idea, but they finally decided they "couldn't resist naming him that," so "Albert Arnold Gore III" went on the birth certificate after his birth October 19, 1982.

When David Frost interviewed Al and Tipper in February, 1988, the conversation turned to the children and the Gore family structure.[2]

"Would you say that your husband is head of the household?" Frost asked Tipper.

"I think we're co-heads," she replied, "co-chairmen, ultimately to a certain extent."

Al Gore Jr. on horseback

"Co-chairman," Gore agreed.

"Ultimately—to a certain extent—there's an element of that which I want, frankly. I like to think that we're very equal, not in a traditional way," Tipper said.

Gore emphasized: "Equal, very equal."

*   *   *

His record as a congressman was based on a "common sense" approach to the needs and aspirations of his constituents, who occasionally need a "helping hand" from their government. Even as a congressman, Al Gore held this view, all the while calling for a strong national defense.

He worked long, closely focused hours as a congressman and, with the investigative techniques he had developed as a news reporter and in law school, became one of the most effective and outstanding congressmen in the history of the body.

Gore has been cited on numerous occasions for his work in the House of Representatives. In 1984 *Washington Monthly* magazine named him as one of the six most effective members of Congress.

He has been named by *NEXT* magazine as one of the one hundred most powerful people in public affairs in the 1980's and in 1983 received the National Kidney Foundation's National Health Advancement Award for his work on the issue of organ transplants.

He was chosen by the Jaycees as one of the "Ten Most Outstanding

Albert III, Al, and Albert Sr.

Young Men of America," and in 1980 was chosen by the Tennessee Conservation League as the League's Legislator of the Year.

In 1982 he was named to the Entrepreneurship Honor Role by *INC.* magazine for his support of small business.

* * *

During the Christmas break of 1982, he sent his family home to Carthage earlier and flew down alone to Nashville, where he rendezvoused with sister Nancy at the airport for the drive to Carthage.

As they did each time they were together, Al brought her up to speed on the children and Tipper and the gossip around Washington. Then the talk turned to the gifts each had for Pauline Gore.

"What do you have Mother for Christmas this year?" Al asked.

"I've finally gotten Mother a gift she'll like this year," the former Peace Corps volunteer replied. "Mom's so hard to buy for, but here it is." She proudly pointed to a square, brightly wrapped package in the back seat. "You know how she likes sweets, Al, particularly ice cream, so I got her the latest thing in ice cream makers, an ice cream machine."

Al looked at his sister, then burst our laughing. "Oh, no," he said, "you gotta be kidding. You didn't get that, did you?"

"Sure I did," she replied defensively. "I know Mother doesn't need to eat ice cream, but. . ."

Al, Jim Cooper, Jim Sasser and Howard Baker (1984; photo by Larry McCormack, courtesy *Nashville Banner*)

"You don't understand," Al said as he laughed and picked up the shopping bag he'd brought off the plane. "I got Mother the same thing."[1]

*   *   *

From the development of a comprehensive arms control plan to the authorship of major health and environmental laws to a national leadership role in science and biomedical ethics, Al Gore has established his leadership bona fides. He used his skills as a reporter to probe into health, safety and defense issues which were vital to the public.

He maintained an exceptionally busy and productive legislative pace, all the while maintaining a ninety-five percent attendance record, much above the average. Without question, Al Gore was the most energetic congressman Tennessee has ever had.

During his eight years in Congress, he held 1,600 open meetings, more than any other member in history.

He was named chairman of the Congressional Clearinghouse on the Future, and assigned to the House committees on science and technology and on energy and commerce.

He spearheaded the successful effort to strengthen health warnings on cigarette packages and advertisements. He successfully investigated and recommended action and legislation in numerous health, environmental, energy and communications issues.

As a member of the Oversight and Investigations Subcommittee, he chaired numerous hearings on illegal toxic waste disposal and other issues. Gore chaired the Investigations and Oversight Subcommittee on the Science Committee, where he led investigations into genetic engineering, organ transplants, medical science fraud, super-computer technology, robotics and other science and health issues.

He has had a special interest in the health and welfare of small children, especially those from homes with limited incomes. After he received allegations that the American Home Products Company had produced infant formula that lacked critical nutrients, Gore conducted an intensive investigation, resulting in American Home's recalling a considerable amount of their product. He became the principal sponsor of the Infant Formula Act of 1980, which established minimum nutrition and safety standards for formula.

As a result of the probe he spearheaded into the handling of organ transplants, he became the author and principal sponsor of the National Organ Transplant Act, which established organ procurement organizations and a national computerized network for locating, listing and matching organs and recipients.

After he heard that organized crime had infiltrated the hazardous waste business, he initiated an investigation that resulted in his co-authorship of the Superfund Act of 1980, the federal law that created the primary program to clean up toxic dumps, hazardous waste sites and chemical spills around the country.

He proposed legislation to make generic drugs more available, and led an inquiry into the sale of worthless insurance to uninformed senior citizens, resulting in the passage of the "Medigap" law, which protects older Americans from unscrupulous marketing of worthless insurance coverage.

He's vice-chairman of the Biomedical Ethics Board, has authored an AIDS plan and helped on a plan to aid the homeless, and there's a litany of other health-related and environmental causes he's investigated and championed, together with consumer-related and economic issues.

He did outstanding work in nuclear arms and disarmament, which absorbed his focus after 1980, when eighty-five percent of a group of young girls at a Girl's State program responded in the affirmative to his asking if there would be a nuclear war in their lifetime. After he was assigned to the House Intelligence Committee in December 1980, he began an intensive study of the issue, and developed such an expertise in the field that Paul Nitze, President Reagan's principal disarmament advisor, referred to him as the premier nuclear expert in the Senate.

He and Congressman Norman D. Dicks of Washington and Wisconsin's Les Aspin backed limited MX production in return for a

Gore family

White House promise of greater U.S. flexibility at the strategic arms reduction talks in Geneva.

Although none was ever produced by the Reagan administration because of budget restraints, he secured administration promises that the Midgetman missile, a single-warhead weapon smaller than the multi-warhead MX, would be produced. Gore is convinced that Midgetman would protect the United States from attack without fueling Soviet fears of a U.S. first strike.

He authored a 1984 law which secured viewing rights for two million home satellite television dish owners throughout the nation, and he is the sponsor of pending legislation to eliminate anti-competitive practices in the satellite television programming industry.

He was a leader in the passage of 1983 telephone legislation which resulted in reduced federal access charges for residential and small business telephone ratepayers and increased support for rural, high-cost companies.

Though he enjoyed his years in the House of Representatives, he remained keenly alert for information that Tennessee's senior senator, Howard Baker, might be ready to return to Tennessee and give up the Senate seat that Albert Gore Sr. had once held for eighteen years. That announcement would soon be made.

Albert Sr., Albert III, and Al Gore Jr.; Senate campaign 1984 (photo by Bill Thorup, courtesy *Nashville Banner*)

Victory, U.S. Senate Race, 1984 (photo by Georgia Nell Dukes, courtesy *Nashville Banner*)

Chapter Eight

The principal advantage of a democracy is a general elevation in the character of the people.

James Fenimore Cooper

Tennessee state representative L. H. ("Cotton") Ivy is best known in the four rural West Tennessee counties he represents for a near-perfect Jerry Clower imitation with which he entertains voters and potential voters. But that's not the primary reason he's liked and returned to the Legislature by the down-home folks and the good old boys. He's a down-to-earth, intelligent, pragmatic country politician who cares about his people and knows how to win their hearts and votes. He's also good at persuading them to vote for people he brings around.

Ivy is high on Al Gore and campaigned with him in 1984 to help him win the U.S. Senate seat from which Howard Baker was retiring. He says it was a hot, muggy day, not the best for campaigning, as he and young Al Gore Jr. sped through the rural communities in their quest for potential voters who might congregate in country stores, schools or churches. Keen-eyed, Gore spotted a country softball game in progress, stopped the car and began working the crowd around home plate. After he'd spoken to all the spectators and players, Ivy was ready to move on, but Gore spotted a pickup truck at the crest of a nearby hill with what looked like a man beneath it. He ran up the hill and found a "good ole boy" changing the oil in the truck. He asked the man to come out, but he refused, so Gore knelt down and asked for his vote to send him to the U.S. Senate. Before he gave up on the man, he stuffed a card in the man's cuff and, in lieu of a handshake, squeezed him on the ankle.

Tennessee State Representative
L.H. "Cotton" Ivy

Tennessee State Representative
Mayo Wix

*   *   *

In January 1983, Tennessee state Representative Mayo Wix was about to open a neighborhood meeting for Representative Al Gore in a rural town in Sumner County when a radio flash reported that Senator Howard Baker had announced his retirement from the Senate. He would not seek re-election in 1984, the report said.

Wix recalled that Gore was electrified by the news and seemed preoccupied during the meeting, a condition Wix had never observed in him before. "Go ahead and announce for Senator Baker's seat right here," he urged his friend. Gore smiled, but refused to comply.

From the time of Senator Baker's announcement, however, Gore left little doubt that he would run for the seat. He began lining up grass roots support among rural Democratic courthouse networks and urban party organizations.

The Democratic Party had held all statewide offices in Tennessee from Reconstruction days until 1970, when Republican Winfield Dunn retook the state house for his party. After 1970, with the Republican Party on the upswing in the South, Baker won the post in 1966 and kept it eighteen years, largely because of divisive and brutal Democratic primary contests.

But Gore, immensely popular with Tennessee voters, many of whom felt guilty for having turned the senior Gore out of the Senate fourteen years earlier, staked his claim to the post early and defied any Democrat to take him on. The Republicans had no one to challenge him seriously.

Six weeks after the leader of the Republican majority in the Senate announced his retirement, papers were filed on Al Gore's behalf to form an "exploratory committee" which would seek contributions to finance a campaign to fill the seat.

By this time, too, Gore had also saturated the counties he represented in the Fourth and Sixth Congressional Districts with his open meetings, a tactic he continued throughout the campaign and afterward. During the campaign, he pledged to continue to hold meetings in each of Tennessee's ninety-five counties, and he fulfilled this pledge within four months of taking the position. He has pledged to continue the tradition.

As the Senate race began, money began to pour in to help the popular young legislator. His final contribution total was over $2,000,000, a million more than had been originally expected in contributions.

State Senator Victor H. Ashe, a wealthy, Yale-educated lawyer from Knoxville, was picked by the Republicans to do battle with Gore. Ashe, now mayor of Knoxville, had never been a popular member of the state legislature because of his tendency to needle friends and foes alike, and Tennesseans settled down to do what they enjoy doing in the volunteer state, "voting Democratic." Ed McAteer, a Republican, mounted an independent campaign, splitting the conservative vote and assuring Gore's victory.

Gore campaigned like an incumbent, pointing out his work in the House in safety, health and consumer issues, and seemed to outmaneuver Ashe at every turn. When Ashe called a press conference to accuse Gore of speaking out against busing but voting for it, Gore ignored the charge, responding instead by announcing that Reagan had just signed three of his bills—creating a national organ donor program, requiring stronger warning labels on cigarette packages and strengthening penalties against repeat criminal offenders.

During his son's campaign for the Senate, the senior Gore took a backseat advisory position and did not speak or actively campaign. He also refused to grant any interviews during the campaign, but he was often seen in the audience as Al spoke throughout the state.

Disregarding his father's advice, Al Gore debated Ashe and went on the offensive when Ashe accused him of "coattailing into the Senate" or used the effectiveness issue or the responsiveness issue.

When the debates began, Ashe was overwhelmed. Criticized because he rarely smiled or injected humor into the debates, Gore seized the opportunity when Ashe pulled out a ten-dollar bill and offered it to Gore if he would just utter the name Walter Mondale. Gore laughed, said the words, and promptly donated Ashe's ten dollars to charity in the

Al and Tipper call on Tennessee Governor and Mrs. Lamar Alexander
(1984; photo by Bill Thorup, courtesy *Nashville Banner*)

joint names of Walter Mondale and Victor Ashe. The crowd roared.

While Ashe charged that Gore refused to talk about the issues, Gore
just pointed to his 1,200 open meetings with constituents and to his 98.6
percent voting record in Congress. "The issue," Gore kept saying, "is
effectiveness."

Ashe selected a barking bulldog as his symbol on his ads. Many
Tennesseans found these ads obnoxious, irritating to listen to.

Gore traveled throughout the state and found love and support
everywhere he went. Even many Republicans and Independents
supported his drive for the Senate.

State Representative John Rucker represents Murfreesboro as part
of his district and has known and admired young Gore for years. In
1984, when Gore was campaigning for the Senate, Rucker was
campaigning for re-election. Unbeknownst to each other, both began
"working the line," a group of farmers and cattlemen sitting on a fence
watching the cattle auction at the stockyard. When they reached the
middle, each man extended his hand to the other, then realized what
each was doing, and had a good laugh at the way politicians do things.

                              *   *   *

In the middle of the Senate campaign, Nancy, Al's beloved sister, was
diagnosed with lung cancer. Though she never knew that her illness

was terminal, Gore and the family were devastated as the attractive green-eyed Peace Corps veteran suffered and became weaker and weaker. Pauline Gore had seen Al that devastated only one other time, and that was when his grandparents died. Nancy had always been the staunch, rock-solid friend he could count on regardless. At every opportunity he'd break away to visit her at Vanderbilt University Hospital, where the Gore family had established an outpost at the hospital's hotel, the elder Gore rarely leaving her bedside. On her last day, Al spent several hours alone with her.

Even today Pauline Gore finds it difficult to discuss her daughter's death. Recently interviewed on Nashville television, she said, "It was very difficult for him. We were all very close, although she was ten years older. He thought Nancy was indestructible. Al is a very compassionate person. He grew up very close to his grandparents, and their loss was a very sad thing for him. It has contributed a dimension to him that will be reflected in the kind of person he is and the kind of feeling he has for the people he represents."[1]

On November 6, Gore received sixty-one percent of the vote and carried all but fourteen of Tennessee's ninety-five counties–including Knox, Ashe's home county. Gore received more votes than any other candidate in history had ever received for any of Tennessee's political offices, despite the fact that Reagan was carrying the state with fifty-eight percent. Ashe lost even his home base, the longtime GOP stronghold of Knox County.

*   *   *

Following his victory, Gore was appointed by the Senate leadership to serve on three key Senate committees: the Governmental Affairs Committee; the Commerce, Science and Transportation Committee; and the Rules Committee.

The Commerce Committee has jurisdiction over interstate commerce, communications, science and technology, space research and development and a variety of other areas.

The Governmental Affairs Committee is recognized as the premier investigative body in the Senate.

As a member of the Senate Rules Committee, Gore, who had led the successful effort to broadcast gavel-to-gavel proceedings in the House, immediately began efforts to allow broadcasting of Senate proceedings.

He also continued the work he had begun in the House as the primary congressional sponsor of Health Fairs, the largest privately funded preventive health care program in American history.

When Gore moved into the Russell Senate Office Building in January

1985, he occupied space that had been occupied by former Senators Richard Nixon and John F. Kennedy.

Gore brought his credibility with him into the Senate, where early in 1985 he and fellow Democrats Sam Nunn, David L. Boren and Robert C. Byrd helped produce an agreement with the Reagan administration holding MX deployment to fifty missiles.

The White House was not thrilled with the compromise, but by then its attention was moving to another item on the nuclear arms agenda — the strategic defense initiative (SDI), a space-based defensive missile system. Gore sought a middle ground on this issue as early as 1986, asking the Senate to "exercise caution" on SDI even while admitting that "the political climate. . . is such that a great deal of money is going to be authorized."

To Reagan's $3.7 billion SDI request, Gore agreed to $2.5 billion and sought assurances that work on SDI would not violate the 1972 ABM Treaty. But Gore's funding level was too high for many liberals and too low for SDI boosters, and it lost 59-36.

Of Gore's performance as a senator, publisher John Seigenthaler has said, "I don't think there's a public figure in this state since Estes Kefauver who had the grass roots appeal that Al has."

Nashville Banner political reporter Mike Pigott, who has been covering Gore since that first House race in 1976, says: "One of the ways he developed that appeal is through regular direct contact with voters. Gore has held an estimated two thousand town meetings since 1976. I think they've been important for him from a political standpoint to get out and let them know he's in the state and that he cares about them. We've had some senators in the past that haven't made it home very much and have gotten some criticism, including his own father. I think they [town meetings] are important from that standpoint, and they look good on the resume at election time."

In the Senate, Gore's muckrating urge is still strong. After the space shuttle Challenger crash in January 1986, he was one of the National Aeronautics and Space Administration's harshest critics. Despite his junior status on the Commerce Subcommittee on Science, Technology and Space, he grabbed headlines from more senior colleagues by cultivating his own anonymous contact in the Space Agency, who told him that NASA had sharply reduced personnel devoted to quality control prior to the Challenger explosion. Gore's legislative efforts produced a broader commitment by NASA to quality assurance efforts and its accountability to Congress for those efforts.

In May 1986, Gore was one of nine senators who opposed President Reagan's nomination of James C. Fletcher to return as administrator of NASA, which he had headed in the 1970's. Gore said many of the management problems that contributed to the Challenger crash had begun under Fletcher's earlier tenure.

At the initiative of his wife, Gore has focused congressional attention on rock music lyrics that glorify casual sex, violence and satanic worship. The Commerce Committee held hearings on the subject in 1985, drawing in singing stars to comment on a proposal to put warning labels on music products so that parents can monitor what their children are hearing.

Gore co-authored the 1986 law that addressed problems of high cost and unavailability of insurance coverage for small businesses, local governments and others. He was the principal sponsor and manager of the 1987 legislation authorizing all highway safety programs and legislation authorizing Federal Trade Commission programs. He is the co-author of Civil Service Retirement reforms which became law in 1986.

He has achieved national and international recognition for his contributions to the ongoing debate in the nuclear arms race, and even the Soviets have taken note of his writings and expertise in the field. His credentials were especially enhanced when he was designated to serve on the Senate Intelligence Committee in the Ninety-seventh Congress.

Gore's research has brought him to the conclusion that a first strike by the Soviet Union or the United States would set off a response by the other side that would be catastrophic, probably with world nuclear destruction. Consequently, he authored a comprehensive plan to reduce nuclear arms and eliminate the fear of a first strike by global superpowers. Nuclear strategies are based on the number of missiles that survive an attack, not the number of people. As long as one side can wipe out the nuclear stockpile of the other and still have some missiles in reserve, then there will be instability.

* * *

Don McGehee, a Gore devotee who's a state employee in Nashville, says Gore has a distinctive sense of humor. "He takes things seriously but not himself," says McGehee.

McGehee ran into Gore in Phoenix in late 1986 at a hotel where Gore was to address the national conference McGehee was to attend. Gore had a huge sack under his arm that he wanted to take onto the speaker's platform with him. After several inquired as to the contents, Gore explained that he had just got off a plane from the West Coast and that the sack contained "two beautiful salmon I caught out there." He added, "And nothing's going to stop me until I get these back to Tennessee."

To complicate the matter, the group presented Gore with a fifty-pound inscribed granite marker as a memento of the occasion. Understandably, Gore did not wish to offend the group but obviously could not take both the marker and the fish on his flight back to Nashville. McGehee solved the dilemma by taking the granite marker on to California and other states in the trunk of his car for the next two weeks, freeing Gore to fly home with the two salmon.

"He didn't have the two loaves, but he had two of the five fishes, and knowing Al as I do," McGehee said, laughingly, "I thought he might have a plan to feed five thousand of the homeless with the two he had, and I didn't want to get in his way."

Life again seemed to be settling down for the Gores as 1987 approached. He had settled into the Senate routine easily, Tennessee voters loved him and his family, but others recognized Gore's leadership potential. His life would soon change again.

Al Gore Jr., family and supporters, Carthage, 1987 (photo by Jonathon Newton, courtesy *Nashville Banner*)

Left to Right: Nashville political leaders Jay West, Bill Garrett, Al, and Joe Torrance (photo by David Findley, courtesy *Nashville Banner*)

Al Gore
courtesy *Nashville Banner*)

Al Gore and Rev. Jesse Jackson (1987; photo courtesy *Nashville Banner*)

Al Gore with Nashville music and city leaders Roger Sovine, Nelson Andrews, Henry Hill, and Connie Bradley (photo by Larry McCormack, courtesy *Nashville Banner*)

Chapter Nine

No one who has not had the responsibility can really understand what it is like to be President, not even his closest aides or members of his immediate family. There is no end to the chain of responsibility, that binds him, and he is never allowed to forget he is President.

Harry S. Truman

Fred Martin

After he had announced his candidacy, Gore was faced with the administrative and financial obstacles of mounting a successful national campaign and, at the same time, continuing the pattern of excellence he had developed as a U.S. senator.

He named Fred Martin, a Washington-based advisor to New York Governor Mario Cuomo, as his campaign manager. Martin, 34, an Illinois native and writer with an earned doctorate in history from Harvard, was eager to show that he could run a campaign. He had written speeches in both the 1980 Jimmy Carter re-election try and the 1984 Walter Mondale effort, but the American public had rejected both candidates because they were perceived as weak, men who would not use the force of the presidency to protect America's interests, and nothing that Martin could have written or analyzed could have prevented their defeats. In the campaign of 1988, Martin had certainly allied himself with a different breed.

Gore and Martin were, in appearance, the "odd couple." Martin, slight of build and never without his dark horn-rimmed glasses, initially wore nothing but bow ties but changed to regular ties as the campaign progressed. The Superman-ish looking, heavy muscled Gore, on the other hand, was several inches taller at 6'1", and forty to fifty pounds heavier than Martin.

But both dived into the task of assembling a competent staff and crafting a campaign strategy that would work.

Gore, attempting to avoid improper or unethical practices, refused to use his Senate staff people in his campaign, deciding that the two staffs, the Senate and the campaign, would operate apart from one another as separate entities. Those Senate employees who worked in the campaign office had that time charged against their vacation time—a practice rare in Washington.

By the first of July, Gore had transferred at least seven of his key Senate employees onto the campaign payroll and assigned them to the Gore national headquarters office in Arlington, Virginia.

General Counsel Larry Harrington was named deputy campaign manager. Thurgood Marshall Jr. was named deputy campaign manager for policy. Arlie Schardt and Mike Kopp were named press secretary and assistant press secretary, respectively, while Thomas Sweitzer was named to handle media. Administrative assistant Peter Knight was designated finance director. Gore's long-time friend Johnny Hayes, an insurance executive from Hendersonville, Tennessee, signed on as the campaign's finance chairman and was placed in charge of raising funds.

Debra Callahan was named field director. Richard Nicholson was named New Hampshire coordinator. Ed Lazarus signed on as pollster.

After they felt the national headquarters staff knew its mission and was working well, the effort turned to establishing and staffing local and state Gore offices throughout the country.

Gore and Martin then turned to specifics. Fund raising was a chief concern, and fund-raisers were scheduled throughout the country. Key contributors were identified, and mail and phone solicitation began. They planned the best use of Gore's family members, all skilled and experienced campaigners in their own right, and scheduled their appearances carefully to allow the candidate flexibility in flying throughout numbers of states for airport appearances, fund-raisers, meetings with key political figures and major political rallies.

*   *   *

Though Gore considered himself a national candidate with a national message directed to a like constituency, he and Martin decided that the campaign's main thrust would be toward winning in the states which held their primaries on Super Tuesday, and more particularly, the states whose borders touch Gore's home of Tennessee. Thus "Super Tuesday" became the centerpiece of the Gore strategy.

Second, they would seek endorsement from key Democratic figures throughout the nation, many of whom were also voting delegates through their credentials as "super-delegates" to the national convention in Atlanta in July.

Last, Gore recognized that because of his youth there would be a perception that he was actually establishing his mark for the vice-presidency, and it was decided that there would be no consideration or discussion of that option allowed by anyone during the campaign.

"Super Tuesday" was a concept seized upon by the Democratic Party Leadership Council, whose members recognized that their personal political survival and that of the Party demanded that drastic action be taken before the 1988 election. After Walter Mondale's disastrous 1984 national campaign in which the Democratic Party lost forty-nine of the fifty states, and the recognition that their party had lost four out of five elections since 1964, it was obvious that the Democratic Party's national ticket was the "kiss of death" to local and state efforts.

In plain talk, the Democratic Party efforts led by those like Mondale-Carter-McGovern-Humphrey were far too left of center, and were rejected as extremist by the American public. A candidate whose views are outside the mainstream of American thought cannot be elected to the presidency, as was indicated in the Goldwater, McGovern and Mondale campaigns.

Throughout the country in recent elections, particularly in the South, disenchanted local Democrats had often campaigned for the Republican

Al Gore announces for Democratic Party nomination for Presidency in Carthage June, 1987

ticket, claiming that their party had abandoned them. Many of these were Democrats in the Roosevelt, Truman or Kennedy eras, when presidents provided the nation with leadership that provided a strong defense policy, headed by a president who refused to allow the country to be pushed around; a president not opposed to every weapon system, not too timid or too peace-loving to speak up for America and for freedom; but one who was careful in committing military resources.

Denying that their effort was to launch or back a conservative Southern candidate, the Democratic Leadership Council created "Super Tuesday," the day fourteen Southern states would have their primary elections, changing the dynamic of the nominating process. They also increased the number of "super-delegates" to the national convention. While they claimed that they were giving voters in the participating states a greater voice in selecting nominees and were forcing candidates in both parties to face a broader and more typical electorate, the truth of the matter was political survival of the Democratic Party.

*   *   *

After a heavy schedule of meetings, personal appearances and fund-raisers, Al Gore Jr. came back to his home in Carthage on June 29, 1987, to make a formal announcement of his candidacy and officially begin his campaign.

Governor Ned McWherter endorses Gore as he introduces him June 1987 (photo by Eddie West, courtesy *Carthage Courier*)

It was unusually hot on June 29th in Carthage, but even the heat and the humidity that rolled uptown from the Cumberland River a few hundred yards away couldn't dampen the enthusiasm of the seven thousand people who crowded into the town square.

The crowd was jubilant, happy, in a party mood. Jerry Futrell, a local bank head and Gore's close friend and local campaign manager, had done an excellent job in arranging the event. School buses had been pressed into service to shuttle the crowd into the downtown area, where flags and ribbons were flying. Businesses had their store fronts covered with bright red, white and blue Gore posters, T-shirts, hats, and bumper stickers. Adding to the excitement was a high school band.

After Governor Ned McWherter and U.S. Senator Jim Sasser extolled his virtues, Al Gore walked to the same spot on the steps at the Smith County Courthouse where he had made his first announcement for Congress in 1976. "I want to be your president," Gore told the cheering crowd. "I want you to be proud of me, and proud of America."

"I seek this office to restore the rule of law and respect for common sense to the White House," he said. "Americans in every region and in both political parties have been shaken by the betrayal of public trust, the theft of public money, the shredding of public documents and the dishonesty of public officials," the young senator exclaimed.

He continued, "My first promise to the American people is something

Al Gore speaks to hometown crowd (photo by Eddie West, courtesy *Carthage Courier*)

I can do without any action by the Congress. Any governmental official who steals from the American people or lies to the United States Congress will be fired immediately."

There was thunderous applause from the crowd, which included farmers in bib overalls, mechanics whose pants were still greasy, factory workers from the local shirt factory, bankers, secretaries, clerks and onlookers. They were proud of young Al Gore and of his accomplishments. A local politician predicted that Gore would get ninety-nine percent of the vote in the county.

"My second pledge is to restore respect for common sense in managing the business of government," Gore said.

As he spoke, there were tears in the eyes of many who'd known him

Mattie Lucy Payne

through the years. One of those was a handsome black woman who sat with the Gore family near the Governor and the state's political dignitaries. Mattie Lucy Payne says that she has loved young Al Gore from the time she first met him, when he was three. Retired after teaching for over forty years in the Smith County school system, she feels she practically reared Al Gore.

"He was always fair with everyone, loving, and compassionate," she said. "He never looked at me different because our skins were a different color. He and his family are wonderful, caring people, and he would make the best president the United States has ever had."

The senior Gore was in the House of Representatives when Mrs. Payne first began cooking for the family and caring for young Al and his sister. She often supervised the two Gore children when their parents were called away from Carthage. She described the Gore family as "good people, a religious family highly respected by the local black community."

"Al's prepared himself by outstanding work as a leader in college, the Army, the House and the Senate," Mrs. Payne said. "He shows respect for 'little people,' something I like, and he has the intelligence and integrity it takes to be a leader." Reminiscing, she continued, "He was always a good child. Very industrious, never caused trouble. Even as a young boy, he always wanted to do the right thing. I know. I spent a lot of time with him...."

"His life in Carthage was a big part of his rearing and discipline," she continued. "His father, Senator Gore, insisted that he work in the fields

Al smiles as Kentucky Governor Wallace Wilkinson endorses him

with the farm help, and he'd take up hay, chop corn and tobacco, and
clean fields just like they did. The Senator believed in hard work and
discipline, and insisted that young Al rise early each day. He'd say, 'No
boy of mine is going to lay up in bed while the sun shines.' And Al didn't.
That boy would work, but then he'd play too. He liked to play in the
river. He had a canoe, and fished and boated all over the Caney Fork
River that ran by the Senator's farm.

"Food? Oh, I couldn't fix anything young Al didn't like. At least he always told me he liked it. I spoiled him, I know, but he was so good to be around. I just felt it. His favorites? He liked potatoes, fried or baked, and my fried chicken, especially. He liked green beans, turnip greens, fried corn, squash casserole, cornbread, biscuits, and anything chocolate. I'd make a pan of fudge, and he would eat most of it. He liked chocolate pie, chocolate ice cream, chocolate cookies.

"He liked to bring his school friends here from Washington and Harvard. He had lots of them. They would spend the night and I would cook Tennessee food for them. He had a good sense of humor, but he was a serious-minded child, always. He never had any serious childhood accidents that I knew of. He liked to read all the time, and would bring books when he came home from Washington."

"The farm and Carthage were home for Al," she said.

"I know his heart. He's genuine. I would feel comfortable with him as president, and I want my friends to know how proud I am of him and how I feel about him."

On the steps, Gore continued. "Seventy-five years ago Woodrow Wilson, who represented the ideals of the Democratic Party, a son of the South, ended the long years of internal division and defeat in our party. Fifty years ago, Franklin Delano Roosevelt ended government by the few for the few, that had multiplied the nation's homeless and helpless."

After a pause to wipe the perspiration from his brow, he called the roll of Smith Countians who had lost their lives in Vietnam and pledged an administration that would protect America.

Then he concluded his remarks: "I plan to concentrate on goals that will challenge the best of American minds. . .to build an elementary and secondary education system that is the best in the world, one that will reach 100% literacy by the year 2000. . .to recommit the United States to efficiency and quality and insist on perfectionism, not protectionism. . .to join with cities and states to fight crime, drugs and homelessness. . .to establish a private-public partnership to provide day care for the children of working parents. . .create a more affordable health care system and make new investments to find a cure for AIDS. . .to confront threats to the environment. . .to negotiate with the Soviet Union to end the threat of nuclear arms. . .to heal the divisions among Americans.

"The most serious division is between those who look at the awesome challenges we confront, fear the future and wonder whether or not we have within ourselves to prevail, and those who on the other hand look at the very same problems and feel welling up within them a commitment to work together to rekindle the American spirit and build a future with hope."

Georgia House Speaker Tom Murphy

Former Virginia Governor Charles Robb and Gore (photo courtesy *Nashville Banner*)

The crowd seemed not to believe that he had finished. Then, after a moment or two of stunned silence, there was a long period of applause.

Elated over his reception by Middle Tennessee supporters, Gore visited for a few moments, then hurried for the Nashville airport to continue the campaign. Super Tuesday, he remembered, was only eight months away.

*   *   *

In past campaigns for the House and the Senate, Gore had relied on personal contacts with the voters. He normally stopped at a town, went into the stores, stood at its factory entrances, and walked around the square shaking hands and talking to each voter for as long as he or she wanted. Now, rushing to catch up with the candidates who had started earlier, he learned that he could not campaign that way in a national campaign. Television campaigning was an idea whose time had come in the election process of 1988.

So, in a leased aircraft Gore began traversing the nation, working the Super Tuesday states. Wherever he visited, Gore displayed an uncanny knack for remembering names and events, astounding partisans by greeting them by name.

As he flew into the cities, local politicians came out to be photographed with him. After a brief question-and-answer session before television cameras and local press reporters, Gore flew on to another city, repeating the process.

This process was not original with Gore. Most of the other candidates, usually strapped for funds, followed the same procedure. Generally, the arrival of a major candidate in a city would ensure appearances on the 6:00 and 10:00 P.M. newscasts, which saved thousands of dollars in television advertising.

In addition, the Gore campaign used phone banks, direct mailings and even satellite television. Years earlier Gore had discovered during a congressional investigation how popular satellite television reception had become throughout the United States, and he had purchased time on a Weststar communications satellite known as The Bird. As the satellite orbited the earth 22,000 miles up in the sky, Gore could chat with college students, campaign workers, television anchors and stations. And this relatively inexpensive way of getting his image, voice and message out was available to anyone with a satellite dish.

In Houston the night of the New Hampshire primary, Gore used this technology to talk with two local television anchors, one in New Hampshire, three in Nashville, one in Dallas, and with CBS and NBC.

The next morning Gore spoke to supporters at fifty locations throughout the Super Tuesday states, all available to dish owners, and was able to provide footage for the four national networks and dozens of local television stations at a cost of about $500, coverage that normally would have been financially impossible.

But knowing of, and taking advantage of, existing and inexpensive technology is typical of Gore, who, according to his wife, "reads everything and keeps his eye on the ball."

*　*　*

As the campaign and debates among the Democratic hopefuls continued in 1987 and 1988, Al Gore positioned himself from the first as the lone candidate with a centrist position on most major issues. To establish credibility in states where he was not known, Gore set out to secure the support and endorsements of key federal, state and local political leaders and newspapers. Gore's performance during the debates as a forceful, intelligent professional made the task easier, and his efforts were rewarded with an extraordinarily high number of endorsements.

Gore gave special attention to the eight states whose borders touch Tennessee. He made numerous visits to neighboring North Carolina, Virginia, Kentucky, Missouri, Arkansas, Mississippi, Alabama and

Gore jogs at his farm in Smith County, March 1988 (photo courtesy *Nashville Banner*)

Georgia, reminding voters each time that his home state, Tennessee, was close by, just across the state line.

Gore's appointment of Tennessee Governor Ned McWherter of Tennessee as his Super Tuesday coordinator proved to be one of the better decisions in the campaign. First, the rotund governor told Gore that the campaign needed to go for the votes of "working people—they're the ones who elect people." McWherter, however, began his own search for support among the network of friends and contacts he had made in the Southern political structure in the fourteen years he served as speaker of the House in Tennessee.

In Smith County, Tennessee, Gore's neighbors and friends organized a "Gore for President Gore Corps,"[1] which campaigned extensively for him in Tennessee and Kentucky. James Bass and Jerry Futrell headed the Smith County drive which gave Gore ninety-nine percent of the votes in the county on Super Tuesday.

Gore, greatly impressed with Futrell's work and loyalty, named him as his lone Smith County delegate to the national convention.

"Al Gore's the finest, brightest, and most honest politician I've seen or known in my lifetime," Futrell said. "I've known him and his family for over twenty-five years, and a man of such high character, intelligence, and integrity is destined for leadership."

Governor Wallace Wilkinson of Kentucky gave Gore one of his most significant endorsements. Wilkinson, newly elected to the post in an uphill battle himself, praised Gore, saying, "He's been a great leader in Congress and a great leader in the Senate." Wilkinson said that he based his endorsement of Gore on his electability in the November election, together with his position on education, rural economic development and coal-related issues.

Additional endorsements began to roll in for Gore, especially after he became the first to advertise on the Cable News Network.

In the Wednesday, July 27, 1987, debate among the Democratic contenders, Gore jumped moderator William F. Buckley, whose program "Firing Line" provided a forum for the debate. After Buckley asserted that some estimates of President Reagan's proposed Strategic Defense Initiative, or Star Wars Program, might cost as little as a hundred billion, Gore accused him of drawing his information from "partisan advocates of the Star Wars Program."

In the Sunday, August 22, 1987, debate at Des Moines, Gore ripped Governor Dukakis for not being "specific" in addressing issues, explaining later that "debates are about differences and disagreements and new ideas. If this debate accomplishes anything, I think it'll get us off the generalities."

In a subsequent Des Moines debate on national defense September 27th, and again in Miami on October 5th, Gore stressed his long-standing support of a strong defense policy and a foreign policy that stands up for the nation's interests. Gore pointed out that he was the only Democratic candidate who had supported any aid to the Nicaraguan Contras, favoring low-level maintenance aid while peace negotiations were carried on. Gore took the position that the Sandinistas "can't be totally trusted." He supported American naval action in the Persian Gulf in keeping the sea lanes open, and he supported America's action in Granada. He said his opponents were wrong in underestimating the U.S. military buildup under President Reagan as a force in bringing the Soviet Union to the bargaining table on nuclear arms.

In a major speech at Georgetown University, Gore continued to stress his position to the right of the other candidates on defense. He asserted that a strong national defense was a key element of the Gore candidacy.

Gore continued his emphasis on his defense position into October, when another debate took place in Washington, and one or more of the other candidates always took him to task for his continued references to defense.

On November 7th, he voluntarily disclosed that he had experimented with marijuana while in college, during service in Vietnam, and when he was a reporter. The disclosure caused little stir, probably because of the forthright way in which Gore made the admission.

On November 13th, Gore removed most of his Iowa effort from the state, defending his action by stating that he considered its caucus system of choosing delegates flawed and that he was pursuing delegates in the Super Tuesday states. "If you're going duck hunting, you go where the ducks are," he said. "Forty percent of all the delegates to the Democratic National Convention in July are in the Super Tuesday states and that's where I'm hunting."

Gore's decision to sit out the Iowa caucus and to conduct a limited effort in the New Hampshire primary was questioned by numbers of political experts and members of the media, particularly those of the two states involved.

Gore held to his Iowa strategy, but he did conduct a limited campaign in New Hampshire, where his friend and fellow Tennessean, Johnny Cash, "the Man in Black," appeared with him. The former Grand Ole Opry star and nationally known country music performer sang several songs, after which Gore, a country music fan, said that he and Cash "would walk the line together."

In New Hampshire, the *Concord Monitor,* located in the capital city, endorsed the Gore candidacy, as did Manchester Mayor Emile Beaulieu and state Democratic Party vice-chairman Scott Williams.

Gephardt won the largest number of delegates in Iowa; Dukakis, in New Hampshire.

On January 4, 1988, Gore kicked off his Super Tuesday effort with a number of key endorsements of top political figures in the nation. In Texas, a host of officials pledged support. Texas House Speaker Gib Lewis, elected the top official in the Texas House in 1983 and a state legislator for seventeen years, endorsed Gore and campaigned with him throughout the state.

While he was campaigning with Speaker Lewis and other supporters in Texas in December 1987, Gore finished a speech at the airport in Waco, Texas, and then, accompanied by several Texas politicians and his own staff, took off. Moments later one of the engines caught fire, and the pilot struggled to keep the aircraft under control, finally bringing the craft in for a landing. Undaunted, Gore thanked the pilot, found another aircraft, and resumed the campaign.

Gore was endorsed by a number of political leaders in Texas, not the least importantly by three Corpus Christi lawyers, Ruben, William, and Tony Bonilla. These brothers were active in Hispanic affairs, all having served as president of the League of United Latin American Citizens, which has more than five hundred chapters across the United States. Gore also secured the endorsement of State Representative Juan Hinjosa, chairman-elect of the Hispanic Caucus, another important Hispanic organization.

Since the Democratic National Convention in July was scheduled

Tipper and Al meet children at the middle school near his farm (March 1988; photo courtesy Eddie West, *Carthage Courier*)

for Atlanta, endorsements of top-level political figures in the host state became extremely important. Gore addressed meetings of the Georgia House and Senate and secured the endorsement of Georgia House Speaker Tom Murphy, who became the first major political figure in the state to align himself with Gore's candidacy.

Speaker Murphy became Gore's strongest ally in Georgia, issuing a strong endorsement and hosting a major fund-raiser in Atlanta. Murphy, who traveled extensively with Gore through the state, endeared himself to the young U.S. senator by defending Gore's decision not to campaign in Iowa because "all of us know they are going Republican in November anyway." "I don't think us in Georgia care what they do in Iowa," Murphy continued. "He showed how smart he was by getting out of the cold weather in Iowa."

A few days prior to Super Tuesday, the *Atlanta Constitution* editorially endorsed Gore, stating that his youth at forty was a "boon." "Where most candidates seem to be running for president of the 1980's, Gore is running for President of the 1990's. It's about time."[2]

The editorial referred to Gore's Washington experience and his familiarity with foreign affairs as pluses and pointed out that he "understood the tricky calculus of arms control as no other candidate does" and probed "environment and other scientific issues with large public policy implications as no other candidate of either party has."[3]

Gore's colleague in the Senate, Georgia Senator Sam Nunn, about to depart on a visit to the Soviet Union, issued a statement in which he said he had voted for Gore by absentee ballot because "his views come closest to my own views as to the steps our nation must take to meet our challenges at home and abroad." Senator Nunn's endorsement was timely because the United States Senate's premier defense expert is so highly regarded by Georgia voters and conservative voters throughout the United States.

Gore was warmly received in North Carolina, where he told farmers about his own farm experiences in "planting, suckering and stripping tobacco" and reminded them that he and their champion, U.S. Representative Charlie Rose, had fought numerous battles together against the big tobacco companies. Rose credited Gore with helping in past congressional battles over tobacco, stating, "I've always known Al Gore is with the farmer, the grower, the producer."

After Representative Rose endorsed his candidacy, Gore told crowd after crowd in North Carolina that "I've been on the side of the average working man and woman, the small farmer, not just in commercials, not just in images. Throughout my twelve years in Congress I have been involved in fight after fight against powerful interests." He cited his stands for lower-cost drugs, for adequate labeling of infant formula, for better procedures to allow for organ transplants.

Gore also received key endorsements from Senator Terry Sanford, former Governor James Hunt and Representative James Clark, all powerful political figures in North Carolina. He was endorsed also by several Maryland elected officials, including Representative Tom McMillen, state House Speaker Clayton Mitchell, and state Senate President Mike Miller.

An impressed Edward L. Maggiacomo, a Democratic National Committee member and Gore's state finance chairman in Rhode Island, commented that Gore had broad appeal in his state because he was as much at home with people from Harvard as he was with people from the farm. State Representative Joseph DeLorenzo, his chairman in

Candidate Al Gore, Super Tuesday, 1988

Rhode Island, arranged for Gore to address the state legislature. He was the only candidate of either party to do so.

In Alabama, Gore and the Reverend Jackson won the co-endorsement of the Alabama Education Association. Montgomery City Councilman Joe Reed was instrumental in Gore's receiving the endorsement of the Alabama Democratic Conference, a black organization. Alabama gave Gore key endorsements, including those of Lieutenant-Governor Jim Folsom, House Speaker Jimmy Clarke and Senate President Ryan de Graffenreid. U.S. Senator Howell Heflin of Alabama, a former justice of the Alabama Supreme Court and a member of the Iran-Contra Investigative Committee, endorsed Gore, whom he describes as "a great American."

Nearby, in neighboring Oklahoma, U.S. Senator David Boren said he supported Gore because "Senator Gore is the candidate most attuned to our concerns in the South and Southwest. He is the candidate most committed to national security and he is the candidate best equipped to handle international concerns."

"For our party to remain a majority party and to recapture the White House," Senator Boren continued, "we must appeal to voters in the South and Southwest and to the more moderate voters around the country who make up the bulk of the electorate. I believe Senator Gore is the candidate who can best appeal to these voters."

Gore, who maintains a residence in Arlington, across the Potomac from Washington, was endorsed by an old friend, former Virginia

Governor Charles Robb, a founder of the Democratic Leadership Council, the group which instituted the Super Tuesday primary concept in fourteen Southern states.

Gore endeared himself to a Norfolk audience when he pledged himself to a strong commitment to national defense and attacked his Democratic presidential opponents who would cancel existing contracts under way in the Tidewater on two "super-carriers" to carry through budget cuts. Gore criticized them for taking "positions that I believe are not in tune with the traditions of the Democratic Party under John Kennedy, Harry Truman and Franklin Roosevelt." He defended his own positions on defense, stating that they ensure the United States' ability to negotiate with the Soviet Union from a "position of strength," a keystone of his platform. "Leadership requires strength as well as wisdom," he said. "Franklin Roosevelt understood that....Harry Truman understood it....John F. Kennedy understood it....That is the proud tradition of our party."

In early January 1988, Florida House Speaker John Mills endorsed Gore, characterizing him as "the best opportunity for the Democratic Party, in the most important year for the Democratic party in 20 to 30 years, to regain the White House."

Gore received the endorsement of most of the newspapers in Tennessee. Numerous papers throughout the country praised his candidacy, and the prestigious Washington-based magazine *New Republic* endorsed Gore in its March 7th edition, stating that he was "allergic to the quick fix" and embraced "a strong defense" but was "repelled by the empty flag waving...of the current administration."

Gore spoke before the Mississippi State Legislature, although he generally expected that the state would swing to Jackson because of its predominantly black population.

On January 29th, in a debate at Sioux Falls, South Dakota, Gore stressed that medium range missiles which had been deployed in Europe provided the leverage for the recent INF treaty negotiated with the Soviets by the Reagan administration.

On February 10th, Representative Richard Gephardt's campaign manager, Bill Carrick, was quoted as calling Gore and his aides the "phoniest two-bit bastards" he had seen. This was the most visible sign of hard feelings in the campaign to date.

Beginning on February 14th, Gore was satirized for a week in the "Doonesbury" comic strip, where he was dubbed "Prince Albert," a nickname that brought laughter to Smith Countians who had chopped corn and plowed tobacco with the young man.

On February 16th, Gore placed fifth in the New Hampshire primary.

On March 1st, Gore's campaign began to run out of money and was forced to borrow more that a million dollars to purchase television and newspaper advertising for the Super Tuesday primaries.

On March 5th, Gore won in Wyoming—his first victory in the race. "Three days before Super Tuesday is a pretty good time to have your first win," Gore, obviously elated, told a crowd in Roanoke, Virginia. "I've been telling you something was happening out there."

"This is the first level playing field we've had," he said, noting that Wyoming's selection process had not been affected by New Hampshire or Iowa.

"The undecided votes are breaking our way," he predicted.

Gore had seen and felt the mood of the voters in the South. It was obvious that he could win the hearts of Southern voters when race was not the primary consideration in an individual voter's mind.

Another moment of high drama occurred the night before Super Tuesday, when he and members of the press and his campaign were returning to Nashville on a chartered 727. About fifteen minutes out of Columbus, Georgia, the plane's flaps stuck. As the danger mounted, Gore laughed and joked with reporters as he prepared his obituary.

"Things could be worse," he said. "What if Johnny Cash had been on the plane with us. If he had and it crashed, tomorrow's headlines would read 'Johnny Cash and U.S. Senator Perish.'" Gore, almost doubled over with laughter as the crisis mounted, didn't help the situation by reading the veteran reporters a suggested lead-in to the article: "Just as he was poised on the edge of a brilliant victory in the South, Senator Albert Gore's presidential campaign came crashing to the ground."[4]

No one laughed. Even Gore became somber a few minutes later when they landed and saw that both sides of the runway at Columbus were lined with fire trucks and ambulances[5]

March 8, 1988. Al Gore spent Monday night before Super Tuesday with his family on their farm in the Elmwood community. After he had completed his morning jog on Super Tuesday, he and Tipper voted at Forks River Elementary School, where a crowd of their old friends from Carthage, including Olata and William Thompson, had assembled.

While Al and Tipper were at the school, Gore taught Principal Ronnie Scudder's eighth-grade class, which had been studying the 1988 presidential election. "How many of you believe there will be a nuclear war in your lifetime?" he asked the students. As most of the students raised their hands, Gore shook his head and explained how vital world peace is, and the role of the U.S. in securing it. He told the students they should not carry around a feeling of resignation that a nuclear holocaust is inevitable.

In the mock election that followed, Gore won the unanimous vote of the class for president.

After a few minutes with news representatives, Gore left for the Opryland Hotel in Nashville, where he and his family were staying, to receive election reports and to prepare for a victory celebration that night.

As political experts continued to predict the failure of Gore's Southern strategy, the vote tallies began pouring in, and it became apparent in the first ninety minutes that Gore could win up to seven states.

Gore surprised many observers by winning six states outright: North Carolina, Tennessee, Kentucky, Arkansas, Oklahoma and Nevada. But they were to be his last victories. He finished second in five others. Jackson's wins took place in states with heavy concentrations of black voters: Alabama, Georgia, Louisiana, Virginia and Mississippi. Dukakis won Maryland, Rhode Island, Hawaii, Idaho, Texas, Florida and his home state of Massachusetts. Representative Richard Gephardt won only his native Missouri, the bad news foreshadowing his withdrawal from the campaign just days later after a poor showing in Michigan.

"One of these three is going to be the candidate," Bob Strauss, the Democrats' chief backroom operator and former National Chairman, said flatly.

After the returns had made Gore's Super Tuesday victory certain, he and more than a thousand of his supporters listened to rousing country music tunes at the Opryland Hotel and celebrated their amazing victories. Gore's parents were among the crowd that included many prominent Tennessee Democrats that night.

As young Al Gore walked onto the stage, the crowd waved American flags, brandished signs saying "Al Gore for President," and flashed V-for-Victory signs.

He began: "There's no doubt about one thing—this is a Super Tuesday. Today you and I launched a great cause. We're going to put the White House back on the side of the working men and women for a change. . . .We're going to bring the Democratic Party back to the grass roots for a change."

"Today," he continued, "the voters in twenty states have spoken, and here's what they told the country—"

The crowd interrupted with yells of "Al Gore!"

Gore continued, "They've said it's time more American families had the chance to own a home and send their kids to college. They've said it's time to give America's children the best schools on earth, second to none. They've said it's time to have an all out war against drugs, where the money's not cut in half the day it's declared. They've said it's time to have American workers having good jobs at better wages competing effectively with the people of every nation on the face of this earth. They've said it's time for American corporations to invest more here and create more jobs here in the United States for a change.

"And they've said it's time to expand the American economy, not retreat behind walls of protection, remove the unfair trade barriers overseas but fight here at home to make ourselves more competitive and to give more jobs to American workers.

"Tonight we said no to the old way of doing things and to those who said it couldn't be done. Tonight we showed them that it could be done, on Super Tuesday. [Applause.]

"And ladies and gentlemen, tonight we said yes to the people who make this country work.

"In this campaign and throughout my twelve-year career in the House and Senate, I've taken on some of the most powerful interests in this country, polluters and others who've been against the interests of working men and women. I want to take that kind of leadership and dedication and commitment right into the White House and give this country fundamental change. Not just tinkering around the edges, not just a few minor changes on the margins, but fundamental change in the way we educate our children, the way we compete in the world, and the way we create a better standard of living for our children and grandchildren. We're going to do that in this country. [Applause.]

"And let me tell you about this campaign from here on out. This is a fight for the future of the Democratic Party. It's a fight for whether or not we're going to have a viable national party and win the election in November of this year. We can do it. [Applause]

"We have lost four of the last five national elections, twice by votes of 49 to 1. Are we going to take the same tired old formula from 1972, and 1984, and other elections, and go to the voters again?

"This is a contest between the politics of the past and the politics of the future. We need a nominee who can reach out to independently thinking voters and Democratic constituencies, rebuild our Party's coalition, and score a great victory in November. We can do it.

"In 1960, twenty-eight years ago, America made a choice between politics and hope, between easy promises and a call to greatness, between the ways of the past and a new generation of leadership. I believe we're ready to make that choice again.

"In 1960, we had an incumbent Republican vice-president who had been there eight years and promised more of the same. We had a group of Democratic candidates who in the beginning were unknown, and one of them was awfully young. And all of the talk was 'why can't we get Adlai Stevenson to get into this race?'

"You know which state gave the critical vote at the convention to put John Kennedy over the top? It was the state of Wyoming, and last Saturday they got us off on this row [an old country term], and I'm telling you history is going to repeat itself again because in 1960 we went from the oldest president ever to serve as of that time to the youngest president ever elected. And by coincidence this year we have a chance to do exactly the same thing again. [Applause]

"Tonight with this great victory we proved that old politics and old answers will not work anymore.

"It is time for America to move on, and instead of asking what's best for those in the board rooms, for those who already have wealth and power, it's time to ask what's best for the man and woman on the assembly line, behind the typewriter, the small business person, the small farmer, the person at the grass-roots level, that's what our Party's all about, that's why we won this victory. We're going to go and win in November, ladies and gentlemen. Thank you for being a part of this." [Applause]

*   *   *

After his impressive Super Tuesday victories, Gore continued to try to win over independents to his cause and to the Democratic Party. Just before the Illinois primary, he outlined a political career dedicated to the working class during an interview by Leslie Stahl on the CBS program "Face the Nation":

"I've fought against large chemical companies to stop dumping of illegal chemical waste. I've fought against the large drug companies to keep the price of medicine at reasonable levels. I have fought for increases in the minimum wage. I've fought against Reaganomics. I have fought for lower telephone rates, for lower utility rates. A whole series of battles. That's what my career has been all about."

In its endorsement of his Illinois candidacy on Sunday, March 13th, the *Chicago Tribune* said, "The endorsement is offered in the same spirit as our earlier endorsement of Sen. Robert Dole in the Republican primary—in hopes that an underdog with sound judgement and an important message can pick up momentum in Illinois and contest his party's nomination all the way to its convention." [6]Pointing to Gore as the Democrats' best hope to "prevent the Democratic debate from winding down into the staid pronouncements of Gov. Michael Dukakis of Massachusetts and jazzier echo of the class-conscious Mr. Jackson,"[7] the *Tribune* stressed Gore's knowledge of foreign and domestic policy, his proven ability, and touched upon what had become one of the distinguishing marks of his campaign—that he was "the only candidate who can pass for a political moderate and challenge the Republican nominee for conservative votes."[8]

But Illinois belonged to native son Paul Simon, the U.S. senator loved in all parts of the state. In winning, Simon revived a campaign that had to have a home-state victory. With the heavy black turnout in Chicago and other urban areas, the Reverend Jackson took second place. Gore received only five percent of the vote; Gephardt, two percent. Vice-President Bush easily won the Republican primary, as Republican Senator Dole's campaign began to take its last breath.

The campaign moved on to Michigan, where Gore was endorsed by Michigan House Speaker Gary Owen, Senate Minority Leader Arthur Miller, and eleven other Democratic lawmakers. Owen called Gore "experienced" because of his eight years in the House of Representatives and his four years in the Senate. "We need someone who understands Washington," he said.

In Connecticut, West Hartford Mayor Chris Droney supported Gore, stating that much of Gore's fund-raising success could be attributed to the help of Peter Kelly of Hartford, a former Democratic national finance chairman and member of IMPAC 88, an organization of party financiers pledged to electing a moderate Democrat in November.

In late March former U.S. senator and presidential candidate Eugene McCarthy of Minnesota said that Gore was the only candidate who could unify the Democratic Party. In an endorsement reported by the Associated Press, McCarthy said he was doing so because of Gore's experience and voting record on foreign affairs and economic and environmental issues.

The former senator said, "There is no better preparation for the presidency than being in Congress, especially the Senate. I've felt for some time that the governorship is the worst preparation for the presidency. Saying that because you balanced the state budget you can now balance the federal budget...is nonsense."

McCarthy pointed out that the last two presidents, Ronald Reagan and Jimmy Carter, were both ex-governors, and "we've had almost twelve years of what I'd call an amateur presidency."

At perhaps the last opportunity New York Governor Mario Cuomo had to exercise influence in the election process in 1988, Gore met with him on March 21st and sought his endorsement. Cuomo, however, refused to endorse him, describing their meeting as "interesting" and Senator Gore as "bright and deep in the knowledge of government.... [he] has a particular kind of appeal especially attractive to the Democratic Party at this moment." New York Assembly majority leader Jim Tallon, however, did endorse Gore.

After his impressive victory in Michigan, Jackson's candidacy appeared to pick up momentum. Crowds flocked to hear Jackson, an emotional, exciting speaker, in Connecticut and Wisconsin, and he was featured on the covers of both *Time* and *Newsweek*. The news media, however, began asking questions about his connections with Fidel Castro and Yasser Arafat, his radical social and economic proposals, and his judgment, after the attempt he made to inject himself into the Panama situation involving General Noriega.

Dukakis won in both Connecticut and Wisconsin, with Jackson and Gore finishing second and third in both races. Political experts predicted that Gore would finish with less than ten percent of the vote in Wisconsin, but in the latter days of the campaign the polls showed a dramatic swing his way. Early in the campaign, Gore had received the endorsement of the *Milwaukee Sentinel*; but after he came to campaign in the state and addressed a joint assembly of the state Legislature, the *Milwaukee Journal*, the state's largest newspaper, and the *Wisconsin State Journal*, the leading newspaper in the state's capital city of Madison, also endorsed him. He finished with seventeen percent of the vote in Wisconsin.

On March 12th Jesse Jackson won in South Carolina. Gore began to fall further behind after poor finishes in Illinois, Connecticut and Michigan.

Campaigning in Pennsylvania in late March, Gore received the endorsement of Senate Democratic Leader Edward Zemprelli and the five other members of the Democratic leadership. Zemprelli said that Gore "stands alone" among the Democratic candidates "in his commitment to a sound foreign policy and a strong national defense." "Gore alone," he asserted, "has the qualifications, the expertise, the background and perhaps, most important of all, the desire to lead America."

In New York, Gore met with Israeli Prime Minister Yitzhak Shamir and became the first presidential candidate to express qualified support for the Prime Minister's rejection of the Reagan administration's peace proposals for the Middle East. Gore complained that Mr. Shamir's objections deserved a full hearing, not the "short shrift" they had received from the administration.

On April 14th, five days before the New York primary, New York Mayor Ed Koch endorsed Al Gore, stating that he believed in what Al Gore stands for. Koch, however, vented his personal rage at the Reverend Jesse Jackson because of Jackson's anti-Jewish remarks and activities in years past. Though Gore disassociated himself from Mayor Koch's shrill, personal attack on Jackson, the endorsement turned out to be a liability and damaged Gore's candidacy.

On April 19th, Gore finished a distant third in the New York primary, with ten percent of the vote. After the returns were in, he met with Jackson to repair any damage in their personal relationship that may have taken place in the New York campaign.

*   *   *

Surrounded by the Tennessee Legislative delegation, his wife and children, his parents, his staff, and numerous supporters and press and television reporters, Gore, his voice hoarse from months of campaigning, finally announced in Washington, D.C., on Thursday, April 21, 1988, that he was placing his campaign in suspension.

Following a round of applause, he said, "Thank you very much, one and all, for being here. I appreciate your willingness to share in the end of this campaign as many of you shared in the beginning of this campaign. When I declared my candidacy ten months and a million miles ago, I had one goal in view above all: to restore the Democratic Party to its best and truest conditions.

"I have done my best in this campaign to reclaim a heritage once neglected, and I have done my best as time went on, not only to reclaim but to update it. I have drawn freshly in that effort from our roots, from a diplomacy based upon strength. From an economy that creates wealth before spending and from a society that makes a room for all its people.

"Things didn't work out exactly the way I had planned, and now I know how a lot of folks in America feel—*I was doing great until I turned forty.* I lost this race and that is a disappointment, but some things matter to me more than winning: helping my party, serving my country, knowing when to keep fighting and knowing when I've been licked.

"I will not be the Democratic nominee for president in 1988. The nominee is going to be Michael Dukakis or Jesse Jackson. I'm going to do everything I can to help them do what I set out to do and that is, to put a Democrat in the White House this November.

"I will no longer campaign in the hope of winning the nomination. The nominee is going to be and ought to be one of these two men. Technically, I shall remain a candidate for the nomination but only to enable my delegates to go to the convention so they can represent our point of view in our party's deliberation. I want no part of a stop-Jackson or stop-Dukakis movement. The only man I want to stop is George Bush. . . .

"Although we did not win, we can be proud of what we did accomplish. A campaign is more than one man's pursuit of office, it is a cause. We set out to move the Democratic Party toward the center of American political thought. We also spoke out for a new Democratic foreign policy based on standing up for American principles in the world and standing by America's friends.

"Our cause can be posed as a question: 'Will Democrats speak again as we once did for a majority of our countrymen and women, or are we destined to wander in dissent?'

"We've been subjected for eight years to a Republican who quotes our heroes against us. But Franklin D. Roosevelt does not belong to a man who cannot even see the homeless on our streets. Harry Truman does not belong to an administration that passes the buck for their mistakes. John F. Kennedy does not belong to a president whose employees and friends have corrupted the very idea of public service. And not a single one of those Democratic heroes belongs to an administration whose trillion dollars of net debt, all of which will come due for our children and grandchildren, marks the most selfish generation of leadership in all of American history.

"It's time we reclaimed our heroes. It's time we reclaimed our party. It's time we reclaimed the values we have stood for at our best, and it's time we brought those values to the White House.

"It hurts to have come so far and fallen short. But there will be other days for me and for the causes that matter to us.

"When I look back on this race, I will remember what I have learned from this campaign and from my opponents; for at their best they taught me a great deal.

"From Gary Hart I learned that ideas matter and can bring people back into politics. All of us in this campaign were enriched by proposals put forth by Senator Gary Hart. From Joe Biden I learned the importance of grace under pressure. When his campaign was unravelling around him, I saw him conduct the Bork hearings with absolute fairness and honor. Joe Biden put the country ahead of his own political struggles and honors us all as Democrats and Americans. From Bruce Babbitt I learned that virtue can be its own reward. Bruce Babbitt cared less about what people thought than about being true to his principles. That kind of courage is rare and sustained us all.

"From Dick Gephardt I learned that passion in the service of policy is powerful indeed. Dick tapped into people's basic emotions about their futures with an eloquence and energy that Democrats will need to renew. From Mike Dukakis I have learned that after eight years of Reagan and Bush, competence *is* charisma in the eyes of Americans hungry for leadership. Mike Dukakis has run a campaign that Democrats can be proud of. He brings a record of achievement that few Democrats and no Republicans match. And finally, from my friend Jesse Jackson, I learned again two old lessons: first, we are a richer party and a better nation when we break down barriers and fight for justice. Secondly, as Theodore Roosevelt first noted as he spoke about what a bully pulpit the presidency is, a successful president must be both a chief executive and a preacher.

"These candidates, my friends all, are the best teachers in the

U.S. Senator Al Gore Jr.

world. . .and among the best Americans. . . .They are what makes the Democratic Party the best for the future of our country."

And with those words ended the presidential campaign of now forty-year-old Al Gore Jr., the freshman junior senator from Tennessee.

*   *   *

Though Gore's campaign started later than the other candidates', he showed his party and the nation in just a few months why he was among the brightest and best politicians of today's space-age political frontier. His excellence had shown through in the decisive victories he'd won in states where the voters had come to know him, where he'd had an opportunity to shed a bit of his natural stiffness. A case in point was Tennessee, where his sincerity of purpose and integrity of mind and heart had captured his home state's electorate the first time he'd run in a statewide race.

But after the race in Wisconsin, when campaign funds that had been collected at a record pace in a relatively short period had been depleted, when he was unable to purchase television time, it was apparent that his clear, sensible message was not rising above the emotional appeal of Jackson or the financial resources that Dukakis had at his disposal.

At forty, Al Gore has shown that he is a man of depth, a United States senator who understands the challenges of the nuclear-space age and the role America needs to play therein, a compassionate man who believes in and has fought for the average American citizen, but above all, a man of integrity and high honor.

Al Gore's time to lead may not have come in 1988, but it will come, and soon, when America turns to this noble public servant, one born to lead.

The author's favorite photo of Al and Tipper (photo by Georgia Nell Dukes, courtesy *Nashville Banner*)

Notes

Preface

[1]Quoted in John Eisendrath, "The Longest Shot: Measuring Al Gore Jr. for the White House," *The Washington Monthly*, November 1986, p. 49.

Chapter 1

[1]Charles Martin, *Letters from a Headmaster's Study 1949-1977*, ed. Louise D. Piazza (Washington, D.C., 1961, 1986), p. 222.

[2]Gail Sheehy, "Gore—The Son Also Rises," *Vanity Fair*, 51:3 (March, 1988), p. 14.

[3]*Ibid.*

[4]*Ibid.*

[5]*Ibid.*

[6]"Where's Social Security Agents?" *Nashville Scene*, September 16, 1987, p. 4.

[7]The following account is taken from Sherborne's article "Gore sought father's best advice," *The Tennessean*, April 13, 1987, p. A-2. Used by permission.

[8]*Ibid.*

[9]*Nashville Banner*, April 11, 1987.

[10]*Ibid.*

[11]*Lebanon (Tennessee) Democrat*, June 29, 1987.

Chapter 2

[1]*The Tennessean,* April 1, 1948. Used by permission.

[2]In addition to Allen, the couple produced Marion Mountz Gore, born January 17, 1862; James S. Gore, born January 18, 1865; Lemuel Gore, born 1867; Bettie Gore, born about 1871; and John J. Gore, born 1874 (*Smith County History,* Curtis Media Corp., 1987, p. 502). Albert Gore Sr. had an older brother, Reginald, known as Reggie, who died in 1959. They had three sisters, Amanda (Mandy), Betty, and Grace.

[3]Albert Gore Sr., *The Eye of the Storm* (1970), *passim.*

[4]*The Tennessean,* October 25, 1970. Used by permission.

[5]*The Tennessean,* May 12, 1957. Used by permission.

[6]*Time,* CXXX (October 19, 1987), 18.

[7]*Nashville Banner,* November 1, 1971.

[8]Amy Lynch, "Albert Gore Jr.," *Nashville Magazine*, March, 1985, p. 63.

Chapter 3

[1]Correspondence with Nolan Walters, 1988.

[2]*The Tennessean,* May 12, 1957. Used by permission.

[3]*Ibid.*

[4]*Ibid.*

[5]Gail Sheehy, *loc. cit.*

[6]Pauline Gore, *Pauline Gore's Cookbook* (1984).

[7]Correspondence with Nolan Walters, 1988.

[8]*The Albanian* (1965), yearbook of St. Albans School for Boys, Washington, D.C.

Chapter 4

[1]Charles Martin, *op cit.*

[2]The follwoing account is taken from an interview of Al and Tipper Gore by David Frost, Fox TV Network, February 8, 1988.

[3]Tipper's mother was born in Battle Creek, Michigan, in 1925. Her parents, Elmer Joseph and Verda Louise Drummond Carlson, moved to the Washington area in 1937. Tipper's mother had only one sister, Betty L. Pettit, who died several years ago. (Her two daughters, Page and Gail, Tipper's cousins, were in the wedding party when Al and Tipper married in 1970.) When Tipper's grandfather, Elmer J. Carlson, died on July 9, 1958, his widow, Verda, remained in the Arlington home where Tipper grew up. After Tipper and Al bought the home in 1977, Margaret and her mother moved to a nearby condominium, where Margaret

still lives. Verda Carlson, Tipper's grandmother, died December 3, 1987.

[4]David Frost Interview, February 8, 1988.

[5]*Nashville Scene*, September 16, 1987.

[6]MacNeil/Lehrer TV News Report, April 1988.

[7]*Ibid.*

[8]*Ibid.*

[9]Gail Sheehy, *loc. cit.*

[10]Louis Romano, "Tipper Gore, Playing Down the Rock War," *The Washington Post*, March 29, 1988.

[11]Pauline Gore, *op. cit.*

[12]April 1988.

Chapter 5

[1]Correspondence with Nolan Walters, 1988.

[2]MacNeil/Lehrer TV News Report, April 1988.

[3]*Ibid.*

[4]Correspondence with Nolan Walters, 1988.

[5]*Ibid.*

[6]*Nashville Scene,* September 16, 1987.

[7]*Alexandria Gazette,* August 20,1970. Out-of-town guests were Admiral and Mrs. Lewis L. Strauss of Brandyrock Station; Mr. and Mrs. Alex Kapetan of Wayne; Mrs. Reggie Ballard, Mr. Victor Hammer, and Miss Maggie Kaufman of New York City; Dr. and Mrs. Sidney Silverstone of Harrison, New York; Miss Kathleen Barbier of Downes Grove, Illinois; Dr. and Mrs. Armand Hammer of Los Angeles, California; Dr. and Mrs. Martin Peretz of Cambridge, Massachusetts; Mrs. Don Di Spirito of Slippery Rock, Pennsylvania; Miss Lottie Miles and Mrs. Harold Stone of Knoxville, Tennessee; and Mrs. Alfred G. Marks of Lebanon, Tennessee.

[8]*Daleville (Alabama) Sun-Courier,* March 9, 1988.

[9]*Ibid.*

[10]*Ibid.*

[11]*Ibid.*

[12]*Ibid.*

[13]Ibid.

[14]*Nashville Banner,* October 25, 1984.

[15]*The Tennessean,* October 25, 1970.

[16]*Ibid.*

[17]*Ibid.*

[182]*Ibid.*

[19]David Frost interview, February 8, 1988.
[20]Used by permission.

Chapter 6

[1]Chattanooga *Times*, January, 1985.
[2]Used by permission.
[3]*Nashville Scene,* September 16, 1987.
[4]Amy Lynch, *loc. cit.*
[5]*The Tennessean*, April 12, 1987. Used by permission.
[6]MacNeil/Lehrer TV News Report, April 1988.
[7]David Frost Interview, February 8, 1988.
[8]*Ibid.*
[9]*Ibid.*

Chapter 7

[1]*Nashville Banner,* June 23, 1988.
[2]Pauline Gore, *op. cit.*, page 30.

Chapter 8

[1]Pauline Gore, interviewed by Teddy Bart on WSMV-TV, March 1988.

Chapter 9

[1]The "Gore for President Gore Corps," a group of supporters who campaigned extensively for him in Tennessee and Kentucky, included State Sen. Tommy Burks, State Rep. Frank Burk, County Executive C. E. Hackett, Road Commissioner Clyde Shores, Tax Assessor Johnny Caplenor, Circuit Court Clerk Carolyn Grisham, County Clerk Joe Scruggs, General Sessions Judge Jacky Preston, Register of Deeds Carol Gibbs, Sheriff Johnny Bane, School Superintendent Wayne Langford, Trustee Judy McDonald, Mayors James Clay and Roy McDonald, Gordon Oldham, and other Smith Countians.
[2]*Atlanta Constitution*, March, 1988.
[3]*Ibid.*
[4]*Village Voice*, No. 12, March 22, 1988, p. 19.
[5]*Ibid.*
[6]*Chicago Tribune,* March 13, 1988.
[7]*Ibid.*
[8]*Ibid.*

Author's Notes

I especially want to thank Dr. Willine Hall for her exceptional service in editing *Born to Lead*. Willine, a trusted and talented family friend, kept me on track, in the right tense, and provided criticism and praise at the right time in appropriate amounts.

Donna Harris Armistead Rankin deserves special recognition and thanks. She led a host of Al Gore's friends in Carthage and Smith County who provided outstanding assistance on the book. It's easy to see why a youthful Al Gore Jr. selected Donna as his first girlfriend. An outstanding athlete and supportive school leader, she is a compassionate person of outstanding character. My family and I are honored to include Donna and her family as new friends.

Although I was assisted by too many Smith Countians to name, those due special thanks and deep appreciation include Terry Pope, Edd Blair, Gordon Thompson, William and Alota Thompson, Bonnie McKinney, Jerre McKinney, Inez Owens, Mattie Lucy Payne, Eleanor Smotherman, Hallie Smith, and Carol Gibbs, who shared their intimate recollections of Al Gore from his birth to the present. Jack Robinson, Charlene Bass, Dianna Dillehay, Sherrie Hackett, Sherry Bennett, Dalton Minchey, Evelyn and Johnny Caplenor, Sandra Ray, Teresa Clay, Carolyn Grisham, Jacky Preston, Walter King Robinson, Don Clarke, and Jerry Futrell are due special thanks. And thanks to those who did not wish to be named.

Special thanks are due to Eddie West, reporter-photographer for the *Carthage Courier*, who provided photographs, information and friendship.

For their help in providing information and photographs, thanks are due Carol Andrews of the *Lebanon Democrat*; Priscilla Collins,

Jacky Preston and Sandra Ray

Left to Right: Teresa Clay, Evelyn and John Caplenor

a young reporter-photographer on the *Southern Star* of Ozark, Alabama; Nolan Walters of Knight-Ridder; and personnel at the Library of Congress.

Sally Moran of the *Nashville Banner* deserves special thanks, as do Eddie Jones, Irby Simpkins and Jack Gunter. Thanks to Mike Pigott for never failing to return my calls or meet with me. The *Banner* was exceptionally generous with photographs and files.

Personnel of *The Tennessean* could not have been more generous with their time, photographs and recollections of their former colleague at the paper. Those due special recognition are John Seigenthaler, Wayne Whitt, Frank Ritter, Jerry Thompson, Jim O'Hara, Annette Morrison, Chantay Stepoe, Larry Doughtery, Charles Fontenay, Frank Empson and Clay Smith, all outstandingly helpful with their recollections and photographs of their former associate. I am grateful to each.

Special thanks are due the numerous city, state, federal court and agency officials in Tennessee, Virginia, Massachusetts, Georgia and the District of Columbia for their assistance.

I especially want to thank Canon Charles Martin of the Washington Cathedral, who supervised Al Gore from the fourth through the twelfth grade as the most competent and caring headmaster of St. Albans School for Boys in Washington and generously shared with me his recollections.

Thanks are due Betty Israel, Irene Womack, Phil Bredesen, Vicki Oglesby, Bill and Paula Cunningham, Elree Hillin Conard, Doug Henry, John Rucker, Wallace Wilkinson, Bart Gordon, Jim Sasser, Gil Merritt, Jack Robinson, and Lionel Barrett.

Special thanks for his many contributions to Ron Green of Curley Printing – K & S Press and to Mike Walker and Linda Brown, who did the excellent typesetting for the book.

I am also deeply grateful to Frances, my wife of thirty-five years, and to our daughter, Rachel Hillin Wesch, whose help and support were invaluable. Rachel spent long hours typing transcripts of interviews, articles, notes and dictation, and both she and Frances indulged me by reading passages aloud.

Finally, to our children, Jim, Suzanne, Tim, Kelly, David, Rachel and Ted and grandchildren Houston, Rachel Camille, Katie, Ford and Henderson, I hope your lives and those of numerous other young Americans will be enriched by the story of Al Gore's inspirational life.

Hank Hillin

Index